The
RELATIONSHIP
ROADMAP

BUILDING →

MEASURING

← MAPPING

PARTNERSHIPS

STRATEGY →

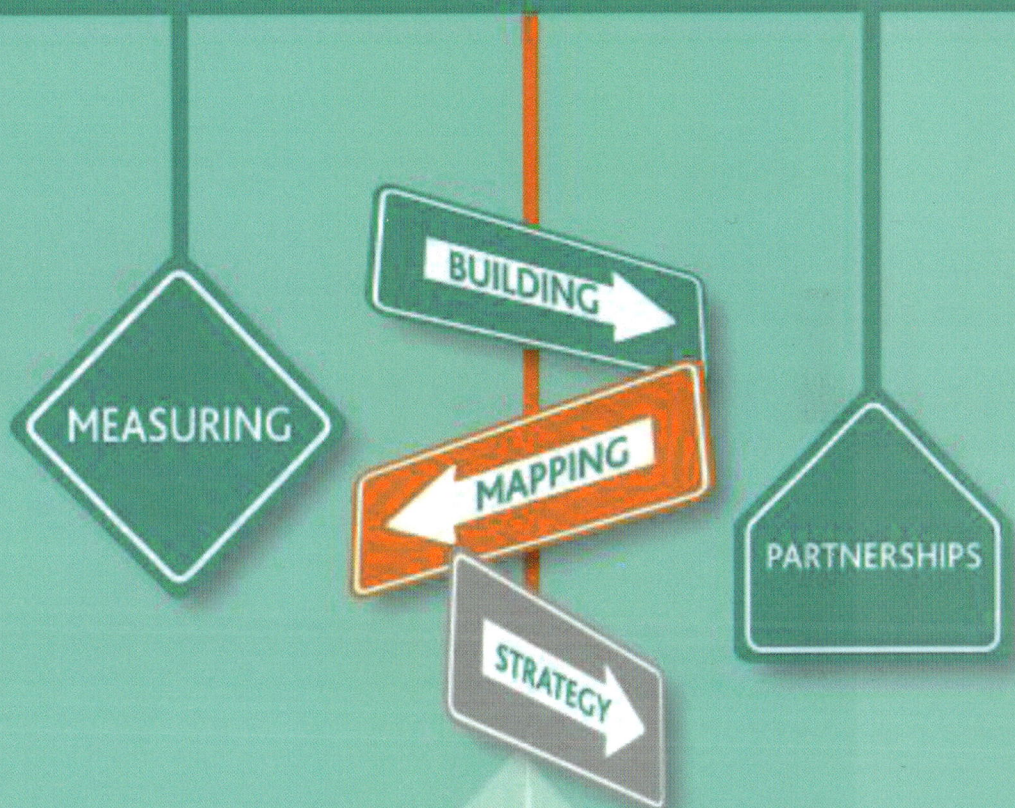

THE
PROFESSIONAL GUIDE
FOR STRATEGICALLY BUILDING AND
MAINTAINING YOUR BUSINESS CONTACTS

PETER M. BEAUMONT

THE RELATIONSHIP ROADMAP

THE PROFESSIONAL GUIDE FOR STRATEGICALLY BUILDING & MAINTAINING YOUR BUSINESS CONTACTS

PETER M. BEAUMONT

ISBN-10: 1492140732

ISBN-13: 978-1492140733

Library of Congress Control Number: **2014918101**

CreateSpace Independent Publishing Platform

North Charleston, South Carolina

Dedication

This book is dedicated to my wife Shelley for putting up with me for so long.

I wish we had met many years before we did, but if that had been the case, as she pointed out, I would have been accused of baby snatching and being the recipient of a potential lawsuit.

Frankly, I keep expecting to come home and find my key no longer works! I love her Dearly!

What's It All About?

You know without customers we don't have any business. And yet, although everyone agrees that business relationships are important no one measures, quantifies or leverages them. This is insane!

So how's this book going to help you with Relationships?

When you finish this book you will not only look at your customer relationships differently but also have a program and process you can start using immediately to improve yours and your companies Relationship Strategy.

To have truly meaningful business relationships, there needs to be a strategic plan rather then relying merely on a transactional approach.

How many Business Plans have you written, reviewed or participated in that have included a plan about key relationships? Not many I'm sure, and yet by not doing so, we miss the very element that we need to get decisions made and products sold and bought!

In this unique book, I introduce the Concept of a Relationship Strategy Plan, which will teach you a 6 Step Process from Relationship Mapping to an integrated Relationship Engagement Plan.

I will explain what it is, how you do it and why it's important. I provide many great examples and provide things you can do straight away to help you develop and track your key relationships. **If you deal with Customers at any level, you need to read this!**

So why should you believe me? Let me introduce myself. Hi, I'm an experienced (read old!) global customer relationship executive and have spent many years helping companies such as Cadbury's, Philip Morris and Coca-Cola succeed and expand through excellent customer relationship management.

I say global because I've worked and lived in 8 countries and travelled to over 80. Few people are aware but apart from new Coke, Coca-Cola have made 2 other mistakes in their illustrious 127-year history. They hired me once, allowed me to escape and then hired me again! They did however finally get their own back!

Using my experiences I founded my own Company called ConnXN in which I consult, advise, mentor, and coach anyone who will put up with me. During the short life of my company (me), I have developed a unique strategic approach to developing and maintaining business relationships and look forward to sharing this approach with you.

I have included a lot of examples to give real texture and authenticity to explain issues.

In order to protect the innocent, although the situations were real as were the companies mentioned, most of the names of the people are false.

Those that were with me during the situations will know who they were. Or will they? Either way I have tried to protect their identities in good and bad examples where it makes sense.

I also hope you will recommend it to millions of people via your Twitter, LinkedIn and Facebook accounts. Enjoy!

Contents

Introduction

Everyone agrees that business relationships are important but very few spend time to plan, measure, quantify, and leverage them strategically in order to increase revenue and profits.

When I started my career I wanted to get into marketing. Don't we all? So I joined Cadbury's[1] in the UK as a sales merchandiser. It seemed like a good idea at the time. Cadbury's provided excellent training and I entered a 6-week program with fellow rookie recruits at the Bournville boot camp just outside Birmingham.

My reasons for joining Cadbury's were as follows: I liked chocolate, they provided some of the best fmcg[2] training and I got a company Ford Escort!

In those days Cadbury's Quaker origins were more obviously prevalent and we were marooned in a small hotel on a Quaker island. The area of Bournville was a model village where Cadbury's was headquartered and had their factories and it was alcohol abstinent.

---

1 https://www.cadbury.co.uk/
2 Fast Moving Consumer Goods

When you are 20 and brought up in Kent where there are more hops grown than apples and you played rugby and cricket; beer is part of your staple diet! Several of us used to sneak out after 'lights out' and partake frequently in late night binges, which always resulted in frequent unmemorable drives home. Drinking and driving then was an acceptable practice and in fact minor scrapes and scratches on the car were pointed out like badges of honor.

The training was a combination of simulated, video recorded sales calls, merchandising exercises, new product drives and relief selling where you took over a sales representatives area for a week. The relief-selling week was the culmination of our training. I always felt this was a high-risk strategy to let these newbies loose on unsuspecting customers who apparently normally had a very professional service.

However, throughout the arduous 6 weeks it struck me that relationships was key to any of the successes we were to have, or not have! It helped me understand the importance of having the right relationships. One particular experience stood out and helped me formulate this view.

My relief selling area was in Cambridge, a very rural and somewhat slow part of the world. At least that was the perspective of a rather flash, suave and modern aspiring executive from London; namely me!

My job was to call on 20 confectionary, tobacco and newsagents (CTN's) per day for the week whilst Barry, the area representative whose area it was, attended some exotic sales conference in the Outer Hebrides. Lucky Barry. I hope he had a good time, because by the time I had finished working his area I'd be surprised if he had any customers left! Shame because he was nice guy!

Anyway, armed with my box of 100 TAM cards (standing for Target, Action, Measurement) I arrived at the hotel on Sunday night and prepared to unleash myself on the poor unsuspecting batch of Barry's customers.

My preparation included looking at previous orders for the last calls and targeting sales for each call I would make. It also included laying out my attire for the next day. In doing so, I selected my best brown London fashion suit which had wide shaped lapels and a contrasting red and beige tie.

The following day did not go well. Nor did Tuesday. After 30 calls since Monday morning, by noon Tuesday I had ONE order! These were customers that Barry obtained orders from with a 90% strike rate for the various Cadbury chocolate and confectionary products.

The UK had a sweet tooth[3] and I KNOW our products were being consumed and it was 4 weeks since Barry did his last visits! Why weren't they ordering? I tried every sales technique in the Cadbury playbook but to no avail!

I drove back early to my hotel in frustration and dejection and sat on the bed with my head in my hands. 5 weeks of training, motivation and enthusiasm in spades and I had ONE order! Something was wrong and I had to change it!

I started to analyze the customer reactions when they were saying no. Then it dawned on me. I wasn't trying to establish a rapport and a relationship with these customers. I was going in with my typical London banter and trying to sell. This was not London and things were more friendly and slow. It was like a New Yorker taking his attitude to Kinosha, Wisconsin, the 289th largest city in the US.

Something had to change. Guess what…it was me! So, I thought about what I was saying when I walked into the outlets. I then went to the full-length mirror on the outside of the closet and stood in front looking at my reflection.

Then I said what I normally said when I walked into these CTN's.

---

3 In 2013 the average Briton devoured 11.2kg (24.7lb) of the stuff - the equivalent of munching through 266 Mars bars.

"Hi, I'm Peter Beaumont. I work for Cadbury's and I'm covering for Barry whilst he's on a sales conference. Lucky for some right? Where's the stock room. I'll take the stock and then come back and tell you what you need! OK?"

This had worked for me before in London…it was my automatic routine! Then I looked at me in the mirror. Pretty cool huh! BUT, maybe my style was a little brash for this part of the world?

Hmm! Maybe I needed to adjust here. I looked at the clothes I'd bought with me hanging in the closet. I tended to buy things I liked in two's, so I had another suit exactly the same as the one I'd been wearing. Fortunately not the same tie!! I picked out a dark blue suit; white shirt and navy blue tie with thin white stripes. I lay them on the bed and then quickly changed. Then I walked in front of the mirror again. More conservative, less out front! Good! I then rehearsed a different approach.

The next morning I was up at 7am, showered, shaved and dressed and sat down to look at the TAM cards for the calls planned for the day. Then I was off. No time for breakfast. Out to the car, jumped in, looked at the map (no GPS systems in those days) and headed to the first call.

I grabbed the TAM card and my sales folder for the first call after parking outside the shop and entered quietly. On seeing a lady behind the counter I said," Hello, my name is Peter Beaumont and I work for Cadbury's. I've been asked to call on you by Barry whilst he's attending a very important sales conference. This is the first time I've done this, as I'm still in training, and actually I'm not sure what to do, but I am here to help you with any information I can provide and take an order for you. Can you help me please? What does Barry normally do?"

Well, I got 19 orders out of 20 for the day! And I learnt a lot… understand who your customer is, adapt to changing circumstances and ask other people what they want. By the way, I also went back to all the

29 customers that did not order with the changed approach and got 24 orders!

I learnt a few important lessons. **I also learnt that we need to think about relationships and people not just outright selling and hoping that one approach fits all!**

I would suggest that we need to be more strategic rather than just transactional with our relationships. What do I mean by that? When I worked with Coca-Cola I used to work closely with colleagues based in Atlanta and several of them were convinced that their relationships were excellent.

This appeared to be loosely based on how much better their handicap was getting on the golf course! However, when I asked them how they would rate the relationship, the answers were vague. They were even more vague when I started asking questions about how they evaluated whether the relationship was with the right people.

We typically form relationships with people we naturally like! But is that the most effective way? You may have a great time and indeed you may think the relationships are good, but how do you know? How do we know it's the right relationship? How do we know it's improving? How do we know we have the right coverage? And how do we capture who has what relationships with our key customers?

Why My Approach to Relationships Works

In all facets of what we do now, we are being held accountable for results, whether it is increased revenues, profits or unit sales.

Seldom if ever do companies look at relationships in the same way. Why not? Because this is a wooly area that most people see as being subjectively driven rather than objectively. **My approach changes that viewpoint and introduces a proper process for measuring this vital area of doing business.**

So What Have I Done?

Over my corporate career I have been fortunate enough to work with some great brands such as Cadbury's, Samuel Smith's, Philip Morris, Coca-Cola and McDonald's and been exposed to some great managers and leaders such as Neville Isdell, Muhtar Kent, John Gillin, Rick Nicholas, Bill Murray, Geoff Bible, Glen Steeves and Jim Skinner.

I have worked in three major roles of Marketing, General Management and Account Management, and as a result have had many relationships and built an impressive network. With this experience I realized that most relationships are based on intuition, like-ability and chemistry but seldom planned or evaluated.

In other words, my experience has demonstrated to me that business relationships tend to be transactionally based rather then planned strategically. Now obviously to have good relationships there have to be things in common as well as high levels of trust and respect, but how many times do we look at all the relationships we have from a 30,000 feet view?

This book is a culmination of my experience and thoughts over the last 30+ years from which I have distilled the essence of what I have learnt and devised a strategic approach to Relationships. Based on a process called Relationship Mapping I will take you, through a process that results in a 6-step guide to devising a Relationship or Customer Strategy Plan.

How Can You Get the Most from This Book?

As the title of the book suggests, it is a Roadmap that will guide you through the relationship minefield and provide a tried and tested process that works.

The goal of this book is to help you get better engaged with the business relationships that really matter for you and get a process that can be consistently used and understood by your management, peers, colleagues and reports.

To do this you can read the book through from start to finish to get a complete picture of how to get a grip on Relationship Engagement. Or you can use it as a reference book by diving into various chapters to help with your own Relationship Strategy. I would recommend you do both!

I have used a lot of examples based on my experience, which help underline various points and serve to illustrate the learning's.

I would recommend you make notes as you progress through the chapters and to help you do this I have included at the end of each chapter some practical things you can put into action immediately. At the end of every chapter you'll also find a summary of the main points.

In addition to this, please visit my website which is full of over 100 business articles I have written on various management areas which will provide you with on going insights and thoughts. Just go to www.ConnXN. net.

How Does this Help You?

This book is written to help you take action NOW! Before you move to the first Chapter, pause and think about what are the issues facing you with business Relationships and what are goals would you like to achieve.

These goals can be general, such as you would like to improve the overall relationship engagement within your area of operation or it may be more specific, such as we need to understand, evaluate and improve our relationships with a specific account or person?

I suggest that you think about them, write them down and refer to them as you read this book. You WILL get a number of new ideas from reading this book, which will result in you being more specific and focused about your Relationship goals.

Let's start!

ONE

RELATIONSHIPS AND WHY ARE THEY IMPORTANT?

"*All lasting business is built on friendship*" – *Alfred A. Montapert (The Supreme Philosophy of Man: The Laws of Life*

Contrary to a lot of views that appear to have surfaced of late, I maintain that good relationships in business are extremely important. And I mean real relationships, not the more tenuous ones formed via Twitter, Facebook or LinkedIn.

The digital world has brought us an element of what I call contact collecting. That is, people don't form real relationships but make contact hits and follow people so they can in turn collect followers.

This apparently is a demonstration to the world of how connected they are. I believe this thinking is just part of a broader view that is taking us down a path of less real relationships and removing real human contact as we hide behind our digital devices with e-mail and texting. And smiley faces or emoticons don't count!!

One such example of this and part of the trend that links with our digital world and the increase in our pace of life is speed dating. For the uninitiated, this is a process where men and women meet in a designated area and are rotated to meet each other over a series of short "dates" usually lasting from 3 to 8 minutes. At the end of each interval, the organizer rings a bell, clinks a glass, or blows a whistle to signal the participants to move on to the next date. At the end of the event participants submit to the organizers a list of whom they would like to provide their contact information to. If there is a match, contact information is forwarded to both parties.

Wow, on this basis we enter relationships?

I am sure it has worked for some but I in the absence of any research to substantiate this, I think we can safely predict that divorce rates will certainly be higher in marriages born of speed dating than those that were spawned over time.

Is it just me, or are we starting to hide behind technology rather than put in the hard work required to build relationships? We are increasingly using technology for tasks we used to handle in person! But it's not just in manufacturing, such as using robots.

Take customer service as an example. I realize, that in the interests of efficiency, productivity and lowering costs by reducing labor payments, that an automated voice-prompted customer service system makes sense. (Does that now become an AVPCSS?).

I am sure the finance guys get all the data and can demonstrate how many customers are processed and how many person hours are saved. Can they also analyze and get data on how many customers were frustrated, hacked off, chased away, lost to a competitor and threw their phone through the window?

I don't care how clever you guys think your automated systems are, they do NOT cover every possibility of what someone wants to say or do and it's as frustrating as heck to navigate! They can't and don't build a relationship with your customer, in fact they can do the very opposite.

We have got so automated that such a mundane thing as answering the phone is not worth bothering about. We claim efficiency when, in fact, it's a ploy to filter and control our day. What? How many live calls do you handle now?

I believe that to form genuine relationships that will stand the test of time, we need to engage with people, listen to people and share experiences.

We tend to form relationships, whether in business or in our personal lives, with people who have similar backgrounds, but it's not just that. It's people that we trust and respect. People we trust and respect are people we want to meet and socialize with. You know what? Business is not that much different. The people that we trust and respect is the people we want to see on a regular basis and risk a relationship and do business with.

So, why are Relationships Important? This seems such an easy question to answer but is it? Let's look at some of the reasons that Relationships matter for business.

One of the most striking quotes I ever came across was one by Mark McCormack, the founder of IMG[4]. IMG started with Mark signing Arnold Palmer in 1960 as his first client and he represented him as his business manager. Following the signing of Arnold Palmer, he also signed Gary Player and Jack Nicklaus, the three greats of golf. IMG went on to become an International management organization that handled the commercial affairs for sports figures and celebrities.

Mark McCormack said...

"All things being equal people will do business with a friend; all things being unequal, people will still do business with a friend"

So, relationships are indeed important and they help build understanding of each other's views. By doing this, they build trust and respect and allow

---

4 http://www.img.com/home.aspx

us greater flexibility in business dealings. For example, a good relationship will allow tests and trials without the risk that if it doesn't work then the business dealings will cease. It allows both parties to re-appraise and look at the situation again.

Good relationships allow mutual understanding and increase and optimize communication. It also allows good and healthy information exchanges and will open doors to getting things done.

Harry Beckworth wrote a really good book called 'Selling the Invisible', in which he talked about what is different about selling a service vs. products. And in his book he says: **"If you're selling a service, you're selling a relationship."**

There have been several books of late that have challenged this and have suggested that, based on the research they had undertaken, that relationships really do not result in sales and that we need to constantly challenge the customer in what he's doing. Furthermore, it suggested that relationship selling was on the decline. One author suggested "….a customer relationship is the result and not the cause of successful selling."

This particular author, of a best selling book I might add, took the stance that the relationships were not so important as the view that you should challenge the customer in every aspect of what he does, and this formed the title of the book.

The theory is that the more we challenge our customer the more we add value and perspective to how the customer thinks. The thinking subscribes to the point of view that this would in fact help to do their job in a way better than they do by opening their thinking to other alternatives.

I agree that creating value is key, but where I differ with this view is that I see it is a part of the relationship building, not necessarily the direct result.

I don't know about you, but if I were a customer and I constantly got challenged on everything I suggested by some obnoxious know-it-all sale person, I wonder how long it would take before I threw them out of my office. Not long. I therefore don't necessarily agree with this notion and do not believe it is that black and white. It's a little like the chicken and egg debate. Which comes first? Now I accept I haven't done justice to a really good piece of work, which involved a great deal of research, and resulted in over 300 pages of content, but that was my main takeaway.

Most books about customers talk about how relationships are key. They must be built first before a foundation can be set to do business. But this can also vary, depending on culture. In David Nour's excellent book called Relationship Economics[5] he says, "During my business trips to Barcelona, Amman and Cape Town, I am often reminded that the rest of the world builds relationships first, before they do business. As businesspeople from North America, we're so focused on the business that if, and only if, that goes well, we'll think about the relationship part." Perhaps this is the reason that we see conclusions as I outlined above, as the authors are taking a US concentric view.

Building relationships is a complex subject and has to take account of a myriad of human emotions, which lie at the core of providing a firm base on which to build a lasting and meaningful relationship.

The reason why business relationships are important is because people are only comfortable working with those they trust and respect. For working with, buying from or collaborating with others to be effective, there has to be trust and respect on both sides. Building this and putting it into a trust bank is the essence of why relationships are important.

As Stephen Covey says in his excellent book "The Seven Habits of Highly Effective People"; "The trust, is the Emotional Bank account, is the essence of Win/Win. Without trust, the best we can do is compromise; without trust, we lack the credibility for open, mutual learning and communication and real creativity."

---

5 http://www.relationshipeconomics.net/NourBook.html

Trust and respect cannot be bought. It has to be earned and it is a result of delivering ideas, helping people, providing great service, thinking ahead and ultimately delivering value and through this process the trust and respect meter needle goes higher.

Over the next few chapters I'll be looking at how you build the relationships and how to be strategic about them and where to focus. Building the right relationships breeds trust, loyalty and ultimately growth together.

When I was working in Vienna, Austria as VP for Coca-Cola on the McDonald's business I had a number of difficult pricing issues, which I describe in more detail in Chapter Eight. But it was not just with McDonald's I had the issues. I had it coming at me from all sides. The Coca-Cola Company Division and Regional offices as well as the Bottlers also attacked me. Why? Because McDonald's didn't think they were getting the best price and The Coca-Cola system felt they weren't making any money from one of the highest volume syrup customers we had. Added to this I had just taken over a newly created role in a new and growing area where all personnel of the customer and my Company were new and changing rapidly. This flux created a difficult environment in which to build trust and respect, as my targets were constantly moving.

In Budapest, Hungary we had some of these issues and it was going to take some time to sort out with the help of Atlanta and McDonald's Division office in Vienna. But Lady Luck played a small hand for me! A fellow called Robert Leechman had been moved within the company to take a key Division role based in Budapest.

A very bright Oxford graduate, Robert and I had worked very closely together in the Middle East and in fact I had played a role as the General Manager of the Coca-Cola Bottler in the West of Saudi Arabia when

Robert was the Country Manager. He had just completed a very successful spell in charge of Coca-Cola's Olympic activities in Sydney in 2000 and had been appointed as President for our Central Europe & Russia business.

I met with Robert before he was actually appointed as he was going through the interview process in Vienna and then several times when he first arrived. As soon as the pricing situation started to get difficult I asked to see him and explained the situation and what it would take to fix.

Because we had worked together, drank together lived on the same island of Bahrain and had kids there, we had understood each other and there was a high level of trust and respect, if not real friendship. Robert gave me the time to sort it out and fully understood the bind I was in and took the bottlers and some of his people off my back.

Over the years we had formed a trust and respect that proved that relationships are as important, and sometimes more so in a case like this, inside your own company as much as outside.

SUMMARY

- Relationships really are important to us and we have to guard against *digitalizing* them into *contact collectibles*.
- They need to be worked at and formed on mutual trust and respect, as they are vital to a successful business.
- Relationships are as important internally as they are externally to allow us to get things done effectively.
- Now I know you want to race on to the next chapter but before doing so, spend a few minutes on the Action section here. I will be placing these little *Action* sections at the end of the chapters to help your thinking in developing an effective Relationship Engagement Process.

ACTION

1. Think about your peers and colleagues as well as external relationships and make a note as who are the key people.

2. Of those key people whom do you currently have a good relationship with and who could be improved?

3. Do you have good coverage at all levels with your major customer?

TWO

PLANNING & EVALUATING OUR RELATIONSHIPS

" **N**etworking that produces long-term business…is not about meeting a lot of people; it's about meeting the right people." – S Michaels

Diversifying Relationships

So, how do we evaluate current relationships and decide whom you should be developing relationships with? I suppose the first question is how do we ascertain whom we should be talking to?

The way that I've approached this and I've learned from experience is you need to map the relationships. You need to layout who are the major players in the organization that you're dealing with and we can start with the core, which is who are the people we're actually talking to, but if we're going to do this effectively we need to look at the whole organization. There may well be people we're missing.

For example, are we speaking to the finance people? A lot of account management people would say, "Why do I need to speak to the finance people? My product's all about marketing." Here are a couple of reasons that may get our attention. Firstly, we need to get bills paid and secondly it may be that we need some help as to how the marketing guys look at their P&L's. We may need a relationship with the finance guy who can actually give us some inside track on how the P&Ls are viewed and give us some advice.

My view is that we need to map the players; the ones that we're dealing with now, but also broaden it out and start thinking about who else could be helping us do better business with our customer. Why?

I would suggest there is a short-term and long-term reason. The short term is because if we don't have a plan for whom we should be talking to and who in our organization should be matched up, then there could be naysayers out there we know nothing about. Ideally, you want everyone at the customer to feel we and our company is worth their investment. A couple of bad apples or non-believers can turn the whole lot rotten, very quickly.

Planning Relationships

But now we go back to planning. Let's talk about planning relationships in a different context. Conferences are great aren't they? Several days out of the office, long flight, hopefully to an exotic location, and all on an expense account. No real accountability, except perhaps either notes taken or feedback provided back to teams the week after. Many people view conferences as a paid-for vacation, perk of the job, or a form of bonus. And yet there can be so much value gained from the investment in attending the right conferences. How so?

First, let's be clear about the sort of conference we are discussing here. Electronic trade shows are an example. The CES,[6] MWC[7] and IFA[8] electronics trade shows used to be the events where new trends were made

---

6 CES: Consumer Electronics Show
7 Mobile World Congress
8 International Franchise Association

and products were unveiled. But lately, some of the big manufacturers have shifted their strategies. Samsung, Sony, and Asus have all started to hold exclusive events of their own to ensure that the spotlight is on their products. Apple, of course, does the same thing.

I would suggest that there are three main reason for attending a conference; networking or building and creating new relationships; building motivation for partner groups, such as dealers, franchisees or sales personnel; and learning about new products and/or services. Hearing Steve Jobs talk, not only motivated and made Apple people proud of the company they worked for, but also enthused people in the entire industry.

I would also suggest that the most important area is networking or building and creating new relationships. Motivation and learning "what's new" are important, but there are other ways of going about it. So, if this is the most important area, why isn't it approached with a lot more pre-planning and indeed evaluation of results? Probably because there is no methodology and it's not the sexy part of the conference. "Anyway, I'll build relationships by drinking in the bar in the evenings!" Well that certainly is one way to build relationships. And if it's part of an overall plan, that's fine! Too often it isn't…it's the only plan. And also too often, the emphasis is on the drinking as opposed to the relationships!

So, how can we do a better job than just turning up to the bar several times and hoping that we can build or improve our relationships? I would maintain that with good preparation, a plan, and tools for measurement that conference can mean more than visits to the bar and a feeling that I was seen and touched flesh of a number of people I know. **Targeting is essential.** In the words of Yogi Berra, "If you don't know where you are going, you'll end up someplace else." So who is likely to be there? Who do you know well and need to know better? Who don't you know well, but feel it would be good for both of you if you did?

I have often used the Relationship Mapping process, to help me literally 'map' out these things. It's a way of getting our head around who are the players and who should I target to meet and what will I discuss with them. Almost more important, who shall I NOT waste time with. This could be for a couple of reasons. First, you may see that person regularly anyway, and thus, you potentially could waste their time. Second, you could be missing our own opportunities to spend time with people we don't ordinarily have the opportunity to talk to. It's always easier to spend time with those we know and are comfortable with rather than pushing the envelope and building new relationships.

When I worked for Coca-Cola on the McDonald's business, I used to attend the McDonald's Worldwide Convention, which was held every two years. Since 2004, all the conventions have been held in Orlando, Florida. They are massive. Between 15-16,000 people of the McDonald's family, or McFamily, gather there to see latest developments, learn about what's going on, and have a good time.

They are entertained, fed and watered at great expense, as well as motivated by various area of the world and country events held by senior management. Beyond being motivated by senior management presentations, they are given exclusive access one evening to a chosen Disney Park area and entertained by a famous star, such as Rod Stewart or Elton John.

My first visit was mind-boggling. Just the sheer mass and scale of the thing is unbelievable. You also realize very quickly how many or how few people you know.

I used to draw up a list of people that I wanted my boss or senior management to meet and spend time with and those that I needed to get to know better. I had that with me during the day and checked it periodically so I would stay on target. I would then review it each evening and check where I was on the plan. At the end of the conference, I would evaluate how well I had done on the overall plan. Plan and measure against plan!

So, is it really worth attending a Conference? It is worth taking time to evaluate how best to build those much-needed relationships. If we believe there is an opportunity to do this at the conference and there is a way to target and reach the people we want to….Then go for it. But be realistic, because if not, then that $5,000 cost could better be used for inviting those people and entertaining them at dinners or special events.

Relationships are often better built when moving discussions away from the normal environment and making things more personal!

Planning in Relationships is not something you come across a lot and for those of us that are married, in particular, know this only too well! Somehow, when we have a customer we know well and have been dealing with for sometime, we start taking them for granted. Planning relationships is the key to a happy and prosperous partnership.

One of my colleagues at Coke, our VP for Western European business, Prill Brewin, had a novel way of ensuring people knew who their opposite numbers were and set up a very creative 'physical' relationship map. She invited McDonald's to the Coke building in Hammersmith, London, as they had just moved in. She titled the invitation event as the 'Big Breakfast' and senior management of both Coke and McDonald's team were asked to attend.

To ensure attendance she of course got both the most senior people in the respective offices to agree to do it, and then once done, everyone would follow. To make it easy and efficient to do, she arranged a bus to pick up the McDonald's executives early at their office and drive them the 35-minute road journey. She arranged for name cards to be set on a long table and she had 'matched' the executives up to be opposite each other as breakfast was brought in and served.

Of course executives being executives they didn't stay in one place very long and soon they were mingling! Management rarely does what they are told to do for very long.

This creative event ensured that both organizations broadened out their contacts and network and strategically they had new people they could contact as a sounding board or for help. It was a masterful concept that forced potential relationships to start. Whether they blossomed or not would depend on the people and their requirements but the platform had been established in a fun yet meaningful manner. A great idea!

Relationship Coverage

What is Relationship Mapping? Relationship Mapping is a strategic plot of the status of relationship strengths and weaknesses with each of your clients. There are two long-term reasons for mapping relationships. They both concern ensuring we look forward and are strategic about our relationships. In the next chapter we will look in more detail at this when we look at developing a Relationship Strategy Plan. In my view, the relationship strategy plan should be an integral part of the overall company business plan. Without it we fail to discuss who will actually help us implement these great business plans!

When I have asked many account management teams how many people they or their company have a relationship with, they have answered 3-5. We need to think wider than this as to be so limiting means missed potential coverage. When I worked for an agency our biggest client was McDonald's. In fact McDonald's was 98% of the revenue and profits for that agency. As such, we had the luxury of being able to ensure we had vertical and horizontal coverage of key management and influencers for our business. But we didn't.

For a number of reasons, we didn't operate like a normal account-centric company, which is unusual really when you think about it as all our proverbial eggs were in one very large basket.

One of the issues with not caring or thinking about coverage is that people change in corporations fairly quickly and if we're being strategic about our relationships engagement, then the people we were dealing with today are not the same ones tomorrow.

A case in point was when a new CEO was named at McDonald's. We had no relationship with him. We had never heard of him and yet he was promoted from within the company.

There is no excuse for negligent relationship engagement and when it occurs it can be very damaging. It especially makes no sense when you only deal with one account and the corporation you are dealing with prefers and tends to promote from within. This is why a strategic approach to Relationships is so important. It looks at the future opportunities rather than just the fire fighting transactional ones.

Another reason for ensuring we have comprehensive relationship coverage for people critical to our success is the horrifying chance they may fall under a bus tomorrow. Now, I'm not suggesting for a minute that's something we would wish for although I have across some situations where that could have been advantageous. Let's just take them out of the mix, but let's suggest for a minute that's not what we're looking at.

Now, without being so graphic, let's just say they leave. If that person should leave the company tomorrow, where is our coverage? Who's going to replace that person and we have to assume they're normally inside the organization. Sometimes they'll come from outside, but one of the reasons for mapping relationships is to understand who might take that person's job so that if we go in in three weeks to see the same person or he tells us by email he's leaving, we have a relationship with somebody else that may be covering that job and there is no big stop in the way that we proceed with our business.

Because relationships take time to develop, we need to be doing them BEFORE the inevitable happens not after.

Lastly on this issue of coverage, this works internally as well as externally. If we have several people that are responsible for key contacts, we better make sure we have coverage for them, in case they go under that same bus, or even a different one. This means making sure that no one has too much control over one account and that others are involved.

Evaluating Relationships

How can we evaluate our current relationships and measure progress for something that is so subjective?

I've got a major account I deal with right now. It's in the QSR[9] business or fast food business where their senior management is changing on a quarterly basis or has been in the last year. Unless we've got good coverage and decided what we're going to do about that, we're going to be completely exposed to in our plan.

What we have done is moved from dealing everyday with the corporate account and moved downstream to developing relationships with the franchisees, which are the guys who will not change overnight. They have a vested interest. They bought the business. They own it and they are the people that would dictate what's going to happen even if the corporation gives guidance and leadership. This way you have a better handle on the final decision makers and so can have an influence on how our business is going to be shaped.

---

9 Quick Service Restaurant

We need filters and we need other people in the process to help us be realistic.

So, evaluation also means measuring, and part of the mapping process I referred to earlier uses a traffic light system where you grade the relationships as to red, where there's work required, yellow, where it's a good relationship, and green, where it's a strong relationship. We go into detail on this and more in Chapter Three.

So how do we decide what is a good or bad relationship? I guess the easy answer to that is if you don't want to meet somebody, or they don't want to meet you, then it's probably a bad relationship. You certainly don't like them.

How do we apply a litmus test for where we are with our relationships? We need a process or methodology to identify our relationship strengths and weaknesses. Well, given that judging subjective areas is a difficult task to start with, we need a framework and classification so that we can construct some form of map.

Visualize a grid system or an Excel spreadsheet in your mind. We're all pretty used to those. I sometimes get concerned about how dependent I am on spreadsheets. It's just the way my brain computes things. It does make me wonder how my brain would interpret things without Excel!

So, where along the X and Y axis you have names of the contacts, both internal and external, and where the cells match you actually put that traffic light system in and can grid it.

At a very quick view of that spreadsheet we can identify where work is required or where we have a strong relationship. I do use a process or methodology.

It doesn't matter whether the account is large or small and in fact, the grid system will work because we can still grade them and classify them.

In fact, I would go one further, which is we can actually use this system to grid and apply the methodology to internal customers. In other words, **who are the people we work with in our own organization and how strong or weak are our relationships there as well, which can matter almost as much sometimes as relationships we have with our external parties or our customers.**

Part of this process for evaluating your relationships is understanding what is a critical relationship and how to define it? Most of the time people don't concern themselves about critical relationships. They just deal with relationships being at all levels. I would suggest to you a *Critical* relationship is, in business terms, a relationship which if you did not have that relationship, would have a huge effect on whether your company continued to do business with their company or not.

That person has such an influential role in the decision making process that we can or cannot proceed with doing business with them.

Evaluating our relationships is an exercise that is very seldom carried out as it is assumed they are OK. Assume is something that never makes sense. The old training definition of ASSUME is something I still love, which is ASSUME makes an ASS out of U and ME! So we should never assume relationships are what they appear to be. We should always evaluate them and then decide what needs to be done to change them.

In the next chapter we will build on this 'spreadsheet' process and look more closely at how to measure our relationships and the ways we can measure how effective we are and should be.

SUMMARY

- We need to evaluate current relationships and have a way of measuring progress with them.
- Relationships need to be planned if they are to be effective, rather than just hoping they will develop in the bar.
- We need to ensure we have sufficient relationship coverage so that if key people left we would not be found wanting.

ACTION

1. Building on what you did at the end of the last Chapter, think of how diverse your current relationships are and who are you missing that you should be engaged with?

2. If a key person in our client's organization or in ours were to leave, have we got coverage and who would those contingency people be?

THREE

MAPPING RELATIONSHIPS

"*Relationship Mapping is a strategic plot of the status of relationship strengths and weaknesses with each of your clients.*"

So now we understand a little bit more about the practicality and science of mapping relationships what about why and when to use them? As we discussed in the last Chapter, we can use them when we want to review how good our company's coverage is within an organization. This could be either an external organization or indeed an internal division of your own company. For example, I came across a requirement for exactly that with a major client of mine recently when their IT Dept. felt that they we're not serving their 'internal customers' as well as they should. What a surprise!

In my experience, this is a fairly common thing. IT Departments frequently do not see themselves as a resource and service to the rest of the company. Shock, horror, I hear you say! Really? They tend to feel they should be revered and can set priorities and policies as they best feel. After all, we are their mercy and without them, and to be fair, our work would be difficult, if not impossible. No access to e-mail, the Internet, PowerPoint etc. But, they are a service and as such they should see the rest of us as their customers. What a radical thought!

So, the IT Dept. felt the relationship map was a great tool to get to understand where they had relationships and where they had no coverage, so that they could indeed treat the people they serviced like customers. And having established that, then they could go to the next level in understanding where they needed to strengthen the existing relationships and by how much.

In other words, is a 'good' relationship sufficient or does that particular relationship need to be 'strong' for the business partnership to operate at its optimum? Other questions they started to ask at this point were what relationships are 'critical'? And how do we define 'critical'? We'll discuss this more in the next Chapter as we create our Relationship Engagement Strategy Plan.

As a result, I ran a workshop and we started mapping their relationships and talking about how to build relationships, and it soon became apparent to them that they were NOT operating like a service or resource and they had no idea who their key 'customers' were.

Let us look now at the process of Building a Relationship Engagement Strategy Plan. There are 6 steps for this process, which you can see in Figure 1.

In this Chapter we will look at '1. Understanding' and Mapping the Relationships as well as

'2. Identifying' the Customer or Decision Influencers. This is where we look at what the current situation or a snapshot of our relationships on a grid. In the next Chapter we will deal with Steps 3-5.

When should we use this great tool? Well the IT situation described just now would be a good opportunity but typically it is when we are in a situation with a client and we realize that we are not making the progress we either should or feel we should! We would also use it when we feel the need to take the business to another level and perhaps offer new products, ideas or services to the customer, thereby potentially needing different contacts than the current ones with whom we work.

Figure 1:

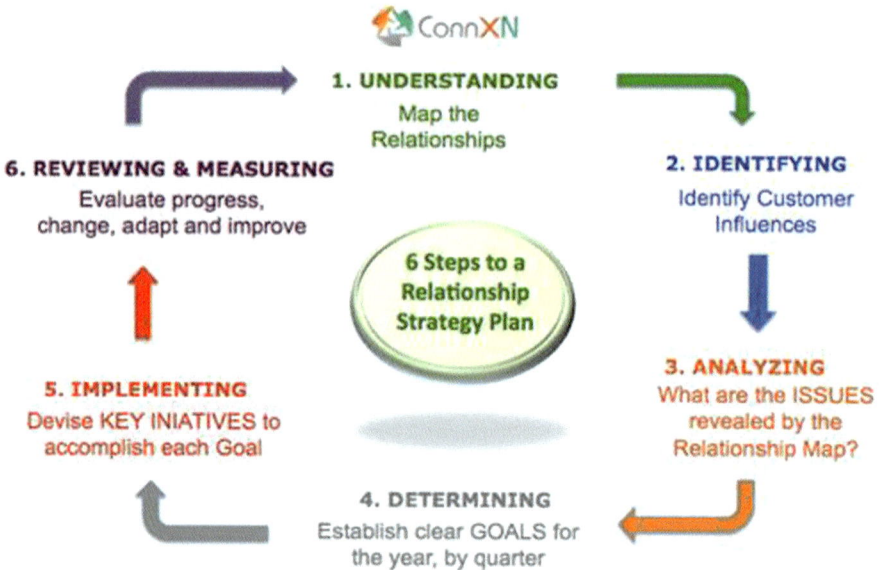

ConnXN

1. UNDERSTANDING
Map the
Relationships

6. REVIEWING & MEASURING
Evaluate progress,
change, adapt and improve

2. IDENTIFYING
Identify Customer
Influences

6 Steps to a
Relationship
Strategy Plan

5. IMPLEMENTING
Devise KEY INIATIVES to
accomplish each Goal

3. ANALYZING
What are the ISSUES
revealed by the
Relationship Map?

4. DETERMINING
Establish clear GOALS for
the year, by quarter

CONFIDENTIAL – Property of ConnXN LLC

In both these situations this is when we start asking ourselves questions such as "Is my contact really looking for the 'win-win'? Should I not have a few other contacts in other Departments? Couldn't my boss be playing a bigger role here? Who else has a good relationship with the key players that could help me? If I or someone else on the account moves on, who will own the relationships? If my main contact gets promoted or leaves, who will take their position and do we have a relationship with them?

This approach to strategic relationship planning is important because it gives us in-depth focus of both the client and our own organizations.

It will demonstrate gaps in our client coverage, as well as providing the opportunity to look at where individuals in our company need to be building relationships.

This approach ensures we are fully customer focused by looking at our horizontal and vertical coverage and involving other parts of our organization. It allows us to see where our management needs to be seen and recognized and where they need to provide relationship air cover for our people on the front line.

Plotting the Map

So how does it work? Imagine that excel spreadsheet I talked about in the last Chapter. Down the vertical or y-axis, you make a list all the contacts you deal with, at the client, such as on Figure 2. It is best to group the contacts by Department, i.e. Supply Chain, Marketing, Finance, Digital, Legal, Operations etc.

Figure 2:

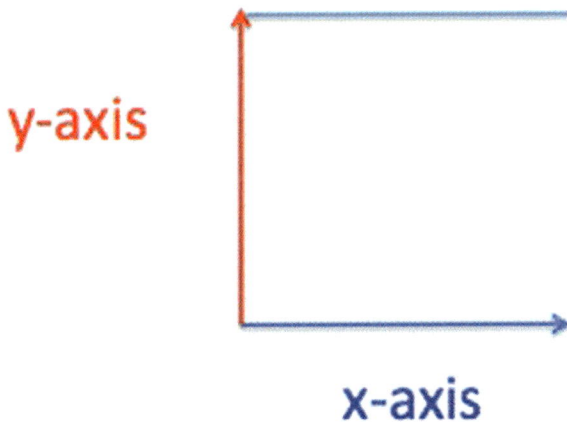

Then, using the top of the horizontal or x-axis, we list our own organization and people that have contacts with the client. When we have listed all the usual suspects, we can start grading the relationships for each client contact with each of our own personnel by using color-coding and letters to represent a graphic snapshot of current client coverage.

Although you can capture various elements of the strengths and weaknesses, it is best to keep it simple and so in my experience the best captures represent 'Strong', 'Good', 'Work Needed,' 'Not Required,' 'Critical Relationships,' as well as who is the 'Primary Contact'. So, we proceed to slotting in names and rating the various relationship levels.

To really capture where we are now and what we need to focus on we need to establish the following:

- The strength of our relationships; by color coding using the traffic light system of 'Red' for Weak relationship, 'Yellow' or 'Orange' for Good relationship and 'Green' for Strong relationship. If a relationship is not required then the cell is left blank or white.

- Next we capture any Critical relationships. These are deemed as a relationship that we MUST have as that person is able to influence senior management and peers views in our favor. NOT to have it would seriously jeopardize our business with the company.

- The Primary relationship: This person is seen as the only person that should receive major communication from your company. There are often a number of overlaps as to who owns the relationships and that's good. You need to have a lot of people involved in a matrix, if you like, of who speaks to whom, but what you do need to do at some point is decide who owns that specific relationship because what you don't want is many company advices going out to the same person. So, this part is really an administrative definition more than a relationship one. Say there's a major announcement within your company that you want to get out to your customer, you don't want it coming from six or seven different people.

As we start filling this out, Figure 3 shows how this might look.

Figure 3:

Account		Our Company							
		PMG Home Office		Host Team/Field					
CONTACT NAME	TITLE/AREA OF BUSINESS	Jeff Richards	AN Other	Joe Doe	Mary Hill	M Jakovic			
Gary Owen	CEO			P					
Rob Van der Persie	COO								
Wayne Rooney	CMO		!			P !			
Sheila van Bosch	Marketing Director								
Stefan Gerrard	Maketing Manager								
Ann Berdych	General Manager								
Venus Williams	Brand Manager				1P				
Aaron Lennon	Product Manager								
Stan Wawrinka	Product Manager								
Mike Dawson	Operations Manager								

We need to be fairly precise about the definitions, and the definitions can vary, but once agreed too, must be used on a consistent basis. Much the same as Performance Review ratings, they have to be consistent in use and not changed to suit our needs. A 'Strong' Relationship could be: **High level of trust, client seeks input and opinion regularly before making decisions, and regular one-on-one meetings (minimum 2-3 per quarter).**

Of course a one-time plot is only the start. All it tells us is where are now. However, to make a difference in our partnerships and ensure we are adding value in building relationships, we need an Action Plan that will positively change the current situation. The place to start is normally with Critical relationships because these relationships should at least be Yellow, and ideally be Green.

This is not a test! We are not trying to look like our relationships are the best vs. others in our team or company. How many times have you heard from colleagues, "Oh we are OK there. I have a great relationship with Tom." Several weeks later we find that we were not in fact 'alright there' as we lost some business, didn't get paid or we lost the account. We need to be totally honest here for this to be meaningful and allow us to plan for better relationships.

I have found that the best way to do this is in a team that is closely associated with the customer so that there are checks and balances in the assessment and differing views that allow us to really explore the subject in depth. The Manager of the team, at a minimum level, should always be present for such an exercise.

Decision Influencers

Having established these critical areas and ratings, we start to build a 'map' of where we are strong and weak with our relationships with an account. However, even if we have a strong relationship with several people, are they the right people to have the strong relationships with? What do I mean by that?

Unless we are strategic and precise about how we measure and appraise our relationships we may indeed have strong relationships, but perhaps with the wrong people. In other words, they may not be the people that can help us influence the health or progress of our business. We need some form of filter that helps us understand whether we are engaging with the people that will benefit us most.

When at Coca-Cola, we were dealing with McDonald's in Germany, and we were trying to get more branding awareness on the translites.[10] This meant that we were trying to get the generic McDonald's cups replaced on the translites with Coca-Cola branded cups.

---

10 Translite: A thin piece of translucent white substrate containing artwork, located behind a clear piece of glass in the menu box. Typically shows menu items, backlit above the counter.

Marketing had bought in to our rationale which was increased incidence of soft drinks through increased branding, resulting in increased profits from soft drink sales. Soft drink sales are mainly an impulse purchase item, unplanned and sought for immediate refreshment. As such, although soda beverages are already a great complement to QSR food, additional triggering of awareness increases incidence and therefore sales.

So our aim was to do that with more branding of Coca-Cola products but we were not able to translate the decision to action. Months dragged on and we were getting more and more frustrated and disappointed. Our local account team was convinced it was going to happen soon. I wasn't! Too much time had elapsed. My team in Vienna went through all the permutations of why things weren't progressing and then we started asking ourselves whether we were talking to the right people. Yes we were, but could they in fact make the final decision?

A conference call with our German team with some uncomfortable questions revealed an hour later that the decision may be being made by Operations people with the budget for translites. Not marketing? Great, we were only talking to 'part' of the decision making process. We had assumed, wrongly, that menu boards and translites were marketing as they promoted the sales and the brand. Wrong. They were seen as an Operations initiative and as such they controlled the budget and ultimately the decisions for lay out on the translites.

Once we realized this, we then identified who was the additional and potentially final decision maker and then drew up a plan to address them. We were fortunate that there was good link between marketing and operations and as soon as we recognized the issue we held joint meetings with them to make our case. A few weeks later we moved ahead with implementation of the initiative. However, the risk here was that if it had continued to drag on, it would have died a natural death. So it's absolutely key to understand who is making those decisions.

In our Relationship Map we have now established the main players and graded our relationships from strong to work needed as well as identifying the Critical and Principal Relationships, so now we need to look at what roles the players are actually playing.

I would suggest to you that customers have four broad roles and although I'm open to suggestions for more, using my experience the four roles are as follows. The first one is a *Budget* role, which translates into "I control the purse strings. I control the money to get what you need. I put my signature on the checks."

The second one would be the *Gatekeeper.* "I don't necessarily use your product, but I could sure as hell come up with a lot of reasons as to why we shouldn't use it. Or "I may not use your product, but I can stop my company using it. It's too expensive. We're not going to pay for it."

The third role would be the one that most people identify with and tend to gravitate towards, which is the *User*, who actually will use our product, service, or idea. They are the people that will benefit mostly, as it will appeal to their needs and requirements.

One of the problems with relationship building is that the User is the only area where people normally play and they forget the other two aspects. Those are the three key roles. There's a fourth, which few recognize or seek out, but can help enormously. That is a *Coach*.

Let's look at these roles in a little more detail and definition. The *Budget* person tends to have the following role sort. They:
- Control expenditure
- Possess the authority to release funds
- Have discretionary use of resources
- And may have the veto power

The *Budget* person will focus on the bottom line and impact on organization and will want to know what the return will we be on this investment and what the potential impact will be on the organization.

The *User* uses or supervises the use of your product, service or idea and will be very involved as they will live with your solution. There will be a very strong bond between User's success and the success of your solution. The User will focus on the job to be done and will want to know how will it work for them in their job or department.

The third role is the *Gatekeeper* as can be seen in Figure 4.

Figure 4:

Probably because of my heritage, my mental image of this function is the Beefeater at the Tower of London in the UK, as seen here. The new King Henry VII[11] the first monarch of the Tudor dynasty formed their official name, the Yeomen Warders[12], in 1485.

The Tudor rose, a heraldic badge of the dynasty, is still part of the badge of the Yeomen Warders to this day. The name Beefeater is of uncertain origin, with various proposed derivations. The most likely proposition is

11 http://en.wikipedia.org/wiki/Henry_VII_of_England
12 http://en.wikipedia.org/wiki/Yeomen_Warders

considered to be from the Yeomen of the Guards' right to eat as much beef as they wanted from the King's table.

In 2011, there were 37 Yeomen Warders and one Chief Warder and they epitomize for me the type of person we encounter with our customers that can't say yes to our entry but can definitely say no and eject us.

These Beefeaters or *Gatekeepers* judge measurable, quantifiable aspects of your proposal and they can't give final approval but they can say "No", normally based on some technical aspect of the project such as creative or technical details. Their interest will be ensuring that specifications are met in their areas of expertise.

The last role we need to understand is that of the *Coach*. This is a very special one and one that is hardly ever sought after. To me, if not pursued and nurtured it is a huge lost opportunity. The Coach's role is to act as guides for bringing the project to fruition as they see the genuine win-win for both parties. They tend to focus on your proposal succeeding and looking at ways to ensure that the solution happens for the benefit of both parties. So let's look at this role in a little more detail.

"All coaching is taking a player where he can't take himself." – Bill McCartney.

What is a Coach and what role does he or she play in Relationship Engagement? Assuming that this is something you feel will add value and results to your strategic partnership efforts, how do you find one? After all, they don't go around with 'Coach' written on their backs like their sports counterparts, or stenciled badges imprinted on their shirt pockets do they?

Coaches can often be people you have identified that can teach you about their business. They feel empathy with you and want you do well because it will help their own company. They may even like you!! They often start as a mentor for you as a client or customer. During the time I worked on the McDonald's business at Coca-Cola I had the good fortune to learn from a number of great Coaches.

The largest market I looked after was Germany. With over 1,200 McDonald's restaurants at the time, the system led a lot of the other smaller European markets and in fact supplied them. Part of my role was to meet with people from the Supply Chain. The Head of McDonald's Supply Chain happened to be based in Munich, Germany. Mike was a native Bavarian and was a friendly, knowledgeable and multi-networked executive. Because of his role, he knew all the senior management within McDonald's Europe as well as many outside.

When I was new to my role, I identified him as being someone that would be open to providing advice and help. In meetings he would not always take McDonald's viewpoint immediately and would be open to both sides of an argument and business proposition. One incident stuck in my mind early on, which made me think I could approach him for help.

My team based in Vienna, Austria, Brita Stiegler, Steffen Kluepfel as well as Werner Melsheimer located in Germany were looking at ways of improving merchandising for our products in the restaurants. To help facilitate our arguments we decided to survey a number of restaurants over a five-day period.

Brita prepared a very thorough survey form and we split into teams and met again at a different hotel in the evenings go through the findings and conclusions. Over the week we ate many Big Macs, consumed too many fries, drank a lot of Coke and enjoyed many liters of German Pilsner in the evenings. We also came up with some interesting results to present to the McDonald's German Board in defense of our proposition.

We made a mistake. We thought we were being smart. By preparing the case we thought we could unveil our findings like a magician from a top hat producing a white rabbit! That's what we did, but in doing so we embarrassed the Director of Operations as we unwittingly called out his team.

He was not amused and although could not question the validity of our findings, he started to question our motive and authority to do what we had without informing McDonald's prior to this. The Head of Supply Chain, Mike, defended our actions in front of the Board and us. He took a far more levelheaded approach and saw the merits in us doing our homework. My take away from that meeting was the following:

- Don't spring surprises on client management
- Seek support for what you are doing prior to going out on a limb
- Seek a Coach before potential confrontations

After the meeting, I decided that I should meet Mike and have lunch with him and thank him. At that lunch, for a variety of reasons, one of which was that he made it clear he was paying, I decided to ask him if he would share his view of the strengths and weaknesses of our company as well as share some of his wisdom about how the McDonald's system operated. What were their objectives, processes and measures?

After the lunch, Mike and I met regularly as he taught me things like the food cost of a Big Mac, the cooking time for Chicken Nuggets and how farmers were selected to grow potatoes. I have always felt that the more you know about your customer's business, the more value you can bring to them with possible insights. And the more value you bring to them, the more you are valued, the more they share, the more you learn and the more value you bring to them and so the circle continues.

I never understood the mentality at an agency I worked for, to just attend meetings on the subject that you are directly involved in and show no interest in anything other than the field in which they operated. This is myopic thinking and does not demonstrate to the client any willingness or commitment to understand, sympathize and be committed to their business.

My discussions helped me enormously. I found that, armed with much more information than I had ever hoped to know, I could hold my own in discussions I had with McDonald's folks on all sorts of subjects. Coupled with travel and being involved in all sorts of new country openings I became an extension of the McDonald's system. More value to them, more value to Coca-Cola.

Mike started as a Mentor and became my Coach. Ultimately he became a trusted friend. When stuck with an issue, I would call him or see him and ask his advice. His reactions and comments were always fair, looked at impartially and predicated a win-win. He would often suggest someone to call, and if I did not know him or her, he would offer to bridge the contact, or host a conference call or luncheon and act as the MC on that call.

One such example was when we were trying to introduce a product into McDonald's Germany and were meeting heavy resistance. The Coca-Cola Company had a fantastic product called Minute Maid Orange Juice, but it really was only sold and known in the US. The brand was not known in Europe at all or very little, but if we could get it into the McDonald's system (for which they had very favorable pricing) then it would help both our sales through McDonald's but also provide us a platform for sampling and introducing the product through other channels in other packages.

The Marketing people were essentially in agreement with the way forward. As I pointed out earlier, Mike was the supply chain responsible for McDonald's Europe and was based in Munich, Germany, which was my biggest market. In the McDonald's business marketing was important, but the supply chain was even more important.

The person working on our juice business at the time was Stefan Thomas and he knew the business very well and he was very tenacious. He had been trying for some time to crack this nut, but to no avail. We decided to try a new approach.

I reached out to Mike because he knew the business really well and we had established a solid relationship. Stefan and I took him out for lunch and said, "This is why we want to do this. We believe that this is the best orange juice around. The fact that you buy Coca-Cola and other products provides economies of distribution as well as good pricing. Therefore, in the supply chain it would be less hassle than going to an outside supplier. Plus you've got a quality symbol on this immediately."

"What I'd like to know from you, and you've always helped me in other aspects, do you think, first of all, we should be doing this? Secondly, if you do, how would we go about it?"

He saw the advantages, or the win-win, for both parties and then advised us over lunch who we should talk to and whom he would help actually setup meetings for. He helped guide us through the process which helped us enormously and six months down the road we actually introduced Minute Maid orange juice into over 1,000 McDonald's stores in Germany.

"True Relationship Engagement is about ensuring all parties get a win. Having a Coach that understands that is invaluable."

Having looked at the four major roles customers can play, it is possible that one person can play more than one role, but no more than two. For example, a contact could be a *User* and have the *Budget* role. That is the most frequent 'double role'.

Budget and *Gatekeeper* role also can combine. *User* and *Gatekeeper* are NOT complementary as that would mean having contradictory motives i.e. I want and need this but here's how I'm going to say no!

In a summary there are four roles as I see it. *Budget, User, Gatekeeper* and *Coach*. Now we have to use these identifying insights on the roles our contacts play by looking at our relationship map and once we have identified and graded our strength's and weaknesses, we need to pinpoint what role our contacts are playing. By the way, this will change. Nothing is constant!

But we need to understand who can help and who can hinder what we are trying to do. Remember as we look at these roles that it's their perception of reality - not yours. The modes represent the Decision Making Influence's perception of their situation and they are not are overall attitudes. They are that individuals attitudes. Yep. It's personal!

We have now established our strengths and weaknesses by color coding and identified the various Customer or Decision Influencer roles. The last phase is to overlay a few more factors such as how much support we have with each individual (Strong or Weak), what degree of influence they have within their own organization (High, Medium or Low) and what mode they may be in (Over confident, Flat, Trouble or Growth). We then have completed our Relationship Map jigsaw or snapshot of our Customer situation.

Our Relationship Map would now look a little like this:

Figure 5:

Account		DECISION INFLUENCES				Our Company						
						PMG Home Office		Host Team/Field				
CONTACT NAME	TITLE/AREA OF BUSINESS	R	I	SW	RM	Jeff Richards	AN Other	Joe Doe	Mary Hill	M Jakovic		
Gary Owen	CEO	UB	L	S	OC			P				
Rob Van der Persie	COO	G	M	W	T							
Wayne Rooney	CMO	U	H	S	S		!			P!		
Sheila van Bosch	Marketing Director	BG	M	W	S							
Stefan Gerrard	Maketing Manager	U	H	W	T							
Ann Berdych	General Manager	C	H	S	T							
Venus Williams	Brand Manager	C	H	S	F				P			
Aaron Lennon	Product Manager	G	M	W	T							
Stan Wawrinka	Product Manager	BG	M	W	S							
Mike Dawson	Operations Manager	G	M	W	T							

As I said earlier, the best way to identify the roles played and which relationships are important is in a team. In my view and experience it has to be a team effort because any relationships that are important to an organization must go through a filter process, both to interpret whether they are work needed, good, or strong.

If we decide individually what we think is a good relationship, we'll always say it's strong because it tends to be human nature. We all have great relationships, right?

That's why you do it in a team because we need a filter process with honest assessments of the strengths and weaknesses of the relationship and who are the major players. Ideally these should be done quarterly as things can change quicker than we'd like. We will look at reviewing more in Chapter Eight.

Priorities

The last part of the Roadmap we need to address is what are the relationships we really need to focus on? Using the Map we need to decide, by person who we should be spending most of our time with. The optimal way to do this is to set Priorities. No more than three but we should, for each of our people interacting with the customer, number cells in the Map, 1,2,3 to signify the importance of where our time should be spent. Obviously, these Priorities will be based on the whether the person is Critical, whether we are trying to move their colors or indeed the role they play as a Decision Influencer. In some cases, as we move up the senior management levels, the priorities maybe only be 1 and 2. This is how our Relationship Map could now look:

Figure 6:

Account							Our Company						
		DECISION INFLUENCES				PMG Home Office		Host Team/Field					
CONTACT NAME	TITLE/AREA OF BUSINESS	R	I	SW	RM	Jeff Richards	AN Other	Joe Doe	Mary Hill	M Jakovic			
Gary Owen	CEO	UB	L	S	OC	2	2	P1	3	2			
Rob Van der Persie	COO	G	M	W	T				2				
Wayne Rooney	CMO	U	H	S	S	1	11	2		P11			
Sheila van Bosch	Marketing Director	BG	M	W	S								
Stefan Gerrard	Marketing Manager	U	H	W	T			3	3				
Ann Berdych	General Manager	C	H	S	T								
Venus Williams	Brand Manager	C	H	S	F				1P	3			
Aaron Lennon	Product Manager	G	M	W	T								
Stan Wawrinka	Product Manager	BG	M	W	S								
Mike Dawson	Operations Manager	G	M	W	T								

Of course a one-time relationship-mapping plot is only the start. All it tells us is where are now. But as we analyze the current picture it will tell us much better where should we focus our time and resources for more efficient results.

To make a difference in our partnerships and ensure we are adding value in building relationships, we need an Action Plan that will positively change the current situation. In the next Chapter we will start our analysis and looking at what we need to do and how we go about it.

SUMMARY

- To 'map' the relationships we need to capture all the main current players with current and required interaction with the client and grade the current relationships with a traffic light coding system which will signify our Strong, Good and Work Needed relationships.
- There are 6 steps to the Relationship Engagement Plan process; Understanding, Identifying, Analyzing, Determining, Implementing and Reviewing & Measuring.
- There are 4 main roles within your client or customer:
  1. *Budget*; Allows funds to be spent on this activity.
  2. *User*; The person who will be most using the product, service or idea that you are suggesting.
  3. *Gatekeeper*; Someone who cannot necessarily approve budget or the use of what's being discussed, but can certainly provide reasons for not proceeding.
  4. *Coach*; A role seldom explored nor utilized that is someone in the customer that gets what you are trying to do and is willing to help you introduce people and broker discussions for a win-win outcome.
- We should identify the **Critical** relationships and the **Principal** ones.

ACTION

1. Knowing what you do about your key business relationships, take some graph paper or using an Excel or Numbers spreadsheet fill in all your key contacts down the left hand side margin (or y axis) and the key people in your company, including yourself, across the top margin (or x axis).

2. Grade those relationships and identify roles that the key contacts play.

3. Prioritize with whom the Team should be spending time with.

FOUR

DEVELOPING A RELATIONSHIP STRATEGY PLAN

" *Strategic Planning is a process by which we can envision the future and develop the necessary procedures and operations to influence and achieve that future."* - Clark Crouch

I have lost count of the number of Business Plans I have drafted, completed and then presented with Coca-Cola and Philip Morris. They are a very necessary business evil. They seem too time consuming, administratively burdensome and non productive; but without them, we do not have any targets, goals or direction. It's a little like playing basketball without the hoops or soccer without the goals. More importantly, they are a great way of communicating to the organization outside of the senior management about what the future holds and what needs to be done to be successful. Now there's a novel idea!

But if used effectively they are like a ships navigation system, a guiding star by which a company's destination is navigated, charted and adjusted over time. Business Reviews are then the key to assessing whether we are on the right course and making adjustments as circumstances require to the chartered route are altered by factors outside our control, such as inclement weather.

Typically the real guts of a business plan are the Objectives (What we want to accomplish), Strategies (Broad areas of focus needed to achieve our Objectives) and Tactics (Specifics and detail of how the Strategies will be executed). **However, what I have never seen in all the plans I have worked on is any reference to Relationships**.

Why is that? I didn't think of it myself for years. And here's the problem. We are so engrossed in the plan itself; we do it in a two-dimensional model. We focus on what we want and how we need to do it. The piece we miss is the third dimension – **whom are we going to do it with?** In other words, who are the people we are talking to as our partners? Are they the right people? Who else are we missing? What are their objectives? What is our current Relationship situation? What are our goals and what initiatives will we take to accomplish them? Our Business Plans and Account Management activities are treated as two separate areas, when in fact they should be integrated.

These critical questions need addressing if we are going to fully execute the Business Plans. It is imperative, in a situation where a company is reliant upon several large customers or clients, that there's a Customer or Client Business Plan in place. It can be a reality filter to the objectives and strategies of the Business Plan and often provide guiding principles as to how the tactics get executed.

"We all know it is critical to have an annual sales, marketing and operating plan. We also need to be cognizant of the different types of relationships you will need to achieve the goals that are laid out in those

plans. A Strategic Relationships Plan will make reaching those goals that much easier!" - David M. Nour.

Let's look again at those 6 Steps necessary to executing a Relationship Engagement Strategy Plan.

Figure 7:

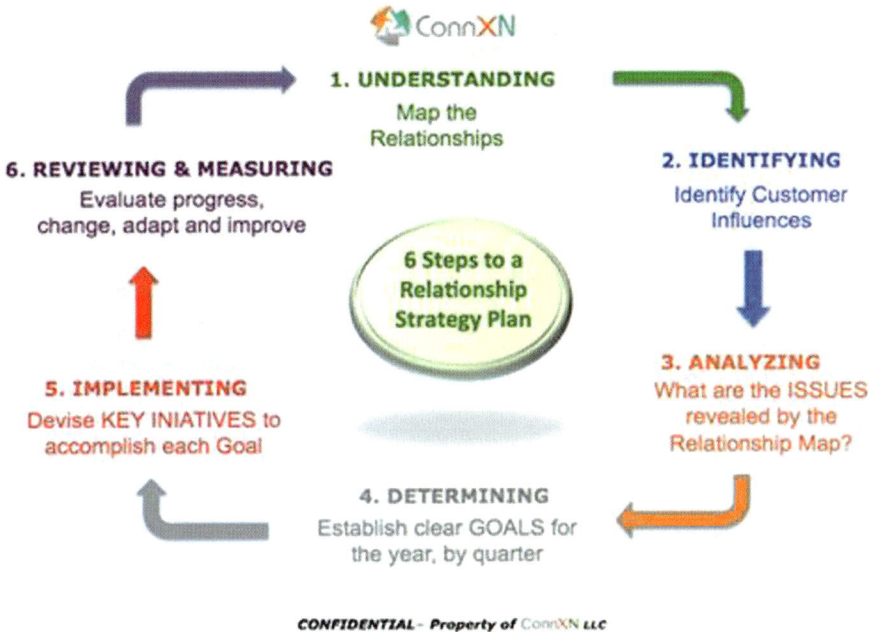

1. Understanding

As we discussed in the last chapter, it all starts with an understanding of who we know and what role all our contacts play, then rating or grading our relationship and mapping these.

2. Identifying

Also in Chapter Three, we looked at understanding where we are strong and weak in our relationships, who is *Critical,* and which are our *Principal* relationships. We then need to identify the really key and meaningful relationships necessary for us to achieve our business objectives. We take a comprehensive look at what we currently know about all of our contacts, and what we don't know. This includes understanding the really key and meaningful relationships necessary for us to achieve our business objectives.

Who are the people that will approve the expenditure? Who will use our service, product or idea? Who will neither approve nor use the service or product but can ensure it is NOT adopted or purchased? As in Chapter Three, we use the *Decision Influencers* to help us ascertain who are the key people with whom we need to have a relationship.

When I was working for an Agency in 2008, we were given two huge projects that would allow us to launch a Digital Services Division. Corporate VP and Head of Sports, Digital and Media for McDonald's, Johan Jervoe placed his confidence in us to deliver two web sites that would provide play and promotional value to their young consumers. We already ran the successful Happymeal.com website in the US and had expanded to Australia and New Zealand.

These two websites were the first large digital promotional projects for us. McDonald's had recently formed a partnership with DreamWorks and the first was 'Kung Fu Panda[13]' released in June 2008. This was another 'DreamWorks[14]' blockbuster in which McDonald's Happy Meal toys would be linked to the main characters of the movie. High hopes were placed on this animated movie and it delivered. With Jack Black, Angelina Jolie, Dustin Hoffman, Ian McShane and Jackie Chan playing the lead voice roles the movie received rave reviews and topped the box office in it's opening weekend, grossing over $60 million.

---

13 http://en.wikipedia.org/wiki/DreamWorks_Animation%22_%5Cl_%22
http://en.wikipedia.org/wiki/DreamWorks_Animation
14 http://www.dreamworksanimation.com/

It was the highest grossing opening for a non-sequel DreamWorks Animation film. What made it challenging for us was that we were given less than three months to create, design, engineer and deploy the website. We had to establish a new team and were working with a largely inexperienced McDonald's team.

The second project was also challenging but we had all learned a lot from the first. This was 'Madagascar 2 – Escape to Africa[15]' which was a sequel. Released in November 2008, we had 5 months this time. Ben Stiller led a talented voice cast and it went on to be at number one at the box office with $63,106,589 with $15,559 average per theater.

As a side note, and to demonstrate how successful they were for DreamWorks, these movies were the number 16th and 17th releases by DreamWorks and Kung Fu Panda is placed 5th and Madagascar 2, in 6th place based on gross billings of $631,744.560 and $603,900,354 respectively.

This was the first time that McDonald's had entered the digital space to support their Happy Meal activities by having a specific website linked to a movie. There had been, and there was a lot of focus on how successful they would be. Having deployed them there was much analysis of how successful they had in fact been and as with any corporation the various interested parties started to surface. We had done a good job and McDonald's were pleased and now we hoped to be able to continue with further sites. The various debates raged of whether this should be done again at all, and then if so, should the sites should be coordinated at HQ or be done locally by areas of the world.

We were very US concentric and hoped that would carry the day, but it didn't. If we had properly mapped the process we would not have been caught with our proverbial pants down. But we didn't and we were! The decision-making process at McDonald's HQ started shifting from

15 http://www.imdb.com/title/tt0479952/

the center to the areas of the world. The HQ budget was coordinated by HQ but largely funded by the areas of the world. Apart from the US and Australia, we, at our agency, had little influence at any depth with any key decision makers in any other areas. We failed to identify the real Users and Economics influences at hand and indeed the Gatekeepers. As a result, we were involved in one more site that was done for Europe for 'Monsters V Aliens' in March 2009 and that was it after that.

The lesson learnt here was that you have to understand the shifting sands and who's making the critical decisions.

3. Analyzing

Having completed our Relationship Map and the snapshot of our current situation, we now have to analyze where all the problems and opportunities exist. Our third step is to analyze our Relationship Map, which now has grading's for level of relationships as well as identifying the various roles and influences within the client. We need to analyze the Map and make a list of all the issues that need addressing. For example evaluate whether the relationships we thought were the right ones to have in step one still the most important ones?

If we do not have the right relationships, then we need to understand where we need additional coverage and where we need to improve and make adjustments in the Relationship Map. If we don't have the right level which are they? This step is similar to the thinking process that goes on in a game of chess. We assess our position and our opponents (the customer or clients organization) and we choose moves that will better cement our standing as well as move the relationship more to a strategic partnership.

A list from this sort of analysis would start something like this:

- We need to help Crispin's relationships improve with Ranger's senior management.

- Ryan to move up the ladder and form relationships with Eric Richards and turn Jeff Radim from 'Red to Green'.
- Mike has High Influence and is a User, but Kevin only has a 'Good' relationship.
- Jeff Radim is a Critical relationships and Linda has a 'Red' grading.
- Tina to utilize her 'green' relationships and influence the customer with them, rather than just saying 'yes'.
- We have too many critical relationships. Who's really critical?
- Who's the potential Coach?
- Cam has no Good or Strong senior level relationships.
- We are not sure of Chia and Linda's relationship standings.
- Consider ways to get Ray engaged with Jack Reacher.
- Need to know Jerry's relationship situation.
- Get Chia, Linda and Sue input and commitment to process and ratings.

As you can see, it's a 'shopping list' of all the things that stand out from the Relationship Map.

4. Determining

The next step is to look at our list of issues and determine what are the key ones we must tackle and change to move our business forward positively. These become our Goals. Now we can't possibly do everything at once. Making a real shopping list for a year would take up more than our usual weekly load. Apart from the issue of where to store everything, it would entail spending more than we typically earn to finance it. So, like a shopping list, we need to do this piece by piece, and determine what we need to do, as we need it.

How do we determine the issues? First of all, locate where the weak areas are and ensure that we've married that up with the roles that those people have to play. Sometimes, we may have a weak relationship, but it doesn't matter because that person isn't in a decision-influencing role that is key to us.

We also need to determine who are the critical relationships and where are the ones that really matter to our business. Once you've decided that, then we can decide how to set the Goals and they become something like, "We need to move that relationship from 'yellow' to 'green'. We need to move that relationship from 'red' to 'yellow'." It's as specific as that.

We need to ensure that Critical relationships are at least 'green', because if they're Critical, they've got to be strong. That's how we set the Goals. **We use the map as the chart or the roadmap for how we move forward.**

Now we need to sort the list by priority and time and then **determine specific goals**.

So using our analysis or shopping list that we generated, let's take the example of "Jeff Radim is a Critical relationships and Linda has a 'Red' grading. The Goal would be for Linda to improve her relationship with

Jeff Radim from 'red' to 'green' by end of 3rd quarter. Here's an example of some Goals:

- Move Crispins's relationship with Walter Toma from 'red' to 'yellow' by end 4th Quarter.
- Move Ryan's relationship with Eric Richards from 'red' to 'green' by year-end.
- Move Linda's relationship with Jeff Radim from 'red' to 'yellow' by end 2rd Quarter.
- Move Ryan's relationship with Jeff Radim from 'red' to 'yellow' by end 3rd Quarter and to green by year-end.
- Move Ray's relationship with Beata Polinsky from 'yellow' to 'green' by end 3rd Quarter.
- Move Ray's relationship with Hisham Jaafari from 'yellow' to 'green' by end 4th Quarter.
- Move Ray's relationship with Jeff Radim from 'red' to 'yellow' by year-end.

These will vary in number depending how much you envisage to complete and they need to be SMART goals i.e. Specific, Measurable, Assignable, Realistic and Time bound. This list of goals becomes the basis of our Key Initiatives.

How do you know goals are realistic? It's a filter process. I've been in account management processes where somebody says, "I'm going to move that from work required, 'red' to 'green', i.e. to 'strong', and I can do that by next quarter."

Relationships don't change overnight so you need somebody in that room to say, "You can't do that. It's just not reasonable. First of all, how are you going to do it? Secondly, how are you going to judge that it suddenly moved to strong?"

What criteria should we use for the Goals? First of all, how important is that role the person plays to our company and can we realistically move it from where it is now or who is the person that's going to move it to and where it should be?

Maybe on the Relationship Map we decide to change the responsibility for that particular relationship to somebody that we haven't normally used to help with that relationship. The criteria we would use is based on who is in the best place to improve the potential relationship.

There's have been times when I've done Relationship Mapping when somebody who has got nothing to do with the customer has actually got a relationship with them that we weren't aware of. If we capture that, then we now have an opportunity, unknown until now, to introduce us via a third party and give us third party credibility to that customer by saying, "I know Peter. He's really good at what he does. Have you spoken to him because I really recommend you listen to what he says because he knows our business and has a great perspective."

Now lastly, on the subject of determining *Goals*, I offer a few words of caution. If you are targeting five accounts or more that you're going to Relationship Map and color code then we need to be careful how this rolls up. Many of our senior management will be involved with more than one account, probably all of them and as such, if we start setting Goals that they move their relationships from 'yellow' to 'green' for 2 relationships on each account, then, with 5 accounts we have 10 relationships that need to be changed. Is that feasible?

That's why we do these exercises in a team and have everyone present so we can be realistic with our targeting. As one CMO one said, "You guys need to go back and be realistic about how many relationships I can turn to 'green' in the next year, and let me give you a clue, it's not in the three months you want me to do it in."

In rolling these *Goals* up we need to ensure the most senior person understands what the expectations of each account group have for those relationships and for them. In some cases, optimism and targets need to be filtered because not all the Goals will be possible to achieve based on the available resources, so someone needs to decide not just which relationships are the most important, but also which accounts are more important than others.

5. Implementing

Our penultimate and probably most important step, is determining how are we going to implement and therefore accomplish the *Goals*. Setting Goals is a fairly simple exercise as they are driven by our list of issues. However, the Goals now need to be converted to Key Initiatives that, like the Goals, are also specific and detailed.

This is a lot more difficult as we have to really think of ways we can improve the status quo in ways that are reasonable and achievable to accomplish those Goals.

Otherwise, with all the other business attention leeches that keep sucking our time, they just will not get done. For example: 'to ensure our CEO has a better relationship with Joe Client, organize two business reviews in the year at which both the CEO and Joe Client are present and get together for an informal dinner afterwards.' Is that feasible and does our CEO agree? Time on the calendar needs to be created, meeting rooms booked, transport arranged and people locked in.

Let's take at look at some examples based on the *Goals* we decided upon that could become *Key Initiatives*:

1. Crispin and Walter meet monthly and discuss geographic, economic update and developments in the industry.
    a. Meetings to consist of:
        o What's happening in the industry
        o High Level Industry Overview (Top-to-Top)
        o Specific Intel Business and ASUS Business
        o How the two can help and/or compliment each other

    b. Crispin to host Walter 2x per year at sports events (or what other interests Walter may have). Crispin will use his sources to get tickets.

2. Ryan to initiate a monthly update meeting with Eric and two special events in the year so that he can spend some quality time away from an office environment learning more about Eric personally and his challenges.

3. Linda to meet with Jeff, and offer him facilities at the agency to see them at work and help his learning's on media. Also offer our own in-house facilities.

4. Ryan to tag with Linda to help develop his relationship with Jeff Radim.

5. Use my strong relationship with Lee Child to set up a luncheon with Beata Polinsky to endorse me and establish regular meetings.

6. Engage with Hisham Jaafari by establishing his goals. I need to get him to some event that would interest him and he feels is special and not something he could do himself.

7. Find out what Jeff Radim is really interested in and engage with him in a couple of events.

The Key Initiatives are what makes all this happen. Without being specific about how to make the Goals a reality and in what way we can deliver those Goals, they just won't be accomplished.

We have now created a Relationship Strategy Plan. A **Relationship Strategy Plan** or **RSP** is our Goals and Key Initiatives. These Goals and Key Initiatives will of course change as people and business circumstances change and this is why need to review them on a regular formalized basis, which we will look at in the next Chapter.

SUMMARY

- To really make a difference in our Relationship Engagement, once we understand the current situation, we need to analyze and determine the areas of opportunities and set *Goals*.
- Setting *Goals* is not enough. We need to implement them by having realistic *Key Initiatives* with which to accomplish the Goals.
- Our *Goals* and *Key Initiatives* are our Relationship Strategy Plan or RSP.

ACTION

1. Having "Mapped" our key relationships, analyze all of them and make a list of the problems and opportunities.
2. Set *Goals* by person that are time bound.
3. Once the *Goals* are set, devise Key Initiatives to accomplish those *Goals* that are specific and measurable.

FIVE

REVIEWING AND MEASURING PROGRESS

Regular Reviews and integration into Business processes

"Measurement is the first step that leads to control and eventually to improvement. If you can't measure something, you can't understand it. If you can't understand it, you can't control it. If you can't control it, you can't improve it." – H. James Harrington.

Our Relationship Strategy Plan is nearly in place. We are ready to start but there are a couple more steps we need to consider before we can embark on the plan. Our last step in the 6-step Relationship Strategy Plan process is Reviewing & Measuring as seen in Figure 8.

A Relationship Engagement Plan, like all Business Plans is only effective and successful when you have regular reviews and build targets into performance reviews so the achieving of Goals has a direct effect on employee's remuneration.

Figure 8:

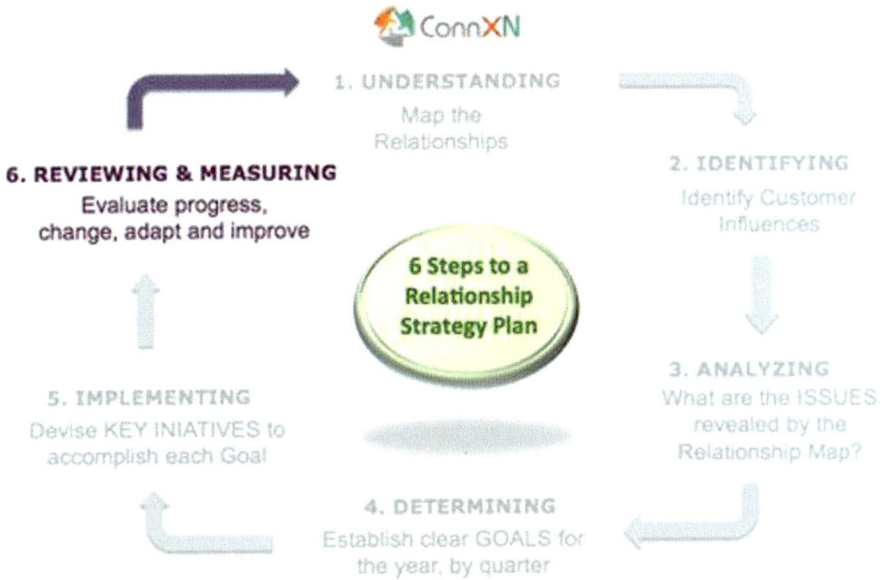

ConnXN

1. UNDERSTANDING
Map the
Relationships

2. IDENTIFYING
Identify Customer
Influences

6. **REVIEWING & MEASURING**
Evaluate progress,
change, adapt and improve

**6 Steps to a
Relationship
Strategy Plan**

3. ANALYZING
What are the ISSUES
revealed by the
Relationship Map?

5. IMPLEMENTING
Devise KEY INIATIVES to
accomplish each Goal

4. DETERMINING
Establish clear GOALS for
the year, by quarter

CONFIDENTIAL – Property of ConnXN *LLC*

Quarterly Reviews

One of the elements normally missing in account management or client or customer engagement is assessing, targeting, and measuring our contacts. What I have learned is that the majority of people treat relationships as transactional. To make Relationship Engagement really effective it has to be strategic and to be strategic about anything, we need to track and measure change. There needs to be some kind of measuring ability.

Therefore, measuring is our last step and is a very important element in ensuring that everyone keeps his or her eye on the ball and that real progress is being made. It is relatively easy to set *Goals*. The trick is to understand how long they will take and devising *Key Initiatives* that really will accomplish the *Goals*.

However, unless we track, adjust and measure progress, then the Relationship or Customer Strategy Plan is for naught. It's a bit like having a Business Plan crafted whilst burning midnight oil, putting it into a wonderful all singing all dancing PowerPoint presentation, delivering it with aplomb and gusto to the Board, getting approval and plaudits and then not looking at it again in a years time. What a waste of time and effort.

The quarterly review should do two things:

- Measure progress on the *Goals* that have been set and ensure we are on track with timing and implementation of the Key Initiatives and

- Based on shifting circumstances, make changes to the current Map and adjust *Goals* and Key Initiatives.

Measuring our Relationship Strategy Plan is fairly easy. Based on the traffic light system, it easy to see how we graduate from 'red' to 'yellow' to 'green'. Either we do or we don't.

Based on the Goals we set, and the examples I provided above, measuring could be done on an individual, a team or a company basis, by aggregating the progress over a quarter, half-year and year. In my experience, the best way to measure progress is to sit down as a team on a quarterly basis and discuss what the *Goals* were and what progress has been made.

Reviews should be at least quarterly. Things change so quickly in business nowadays. You can be dealing the same contacts for quite a while and then suddenly they have moved role, department, country or company.

Quarterly timing for reviews allows sufficient time to allow for the Action Plan to be implemented and to start having an effect. It's also a short enough time to force people to take action and show results.

During these discussions, not only will measuring take place but also real discussions should evolve on what needs to be done to make change happen and be more effective with the relationships. Are we appealing to the right things with this contact? How are they reacting? Do we have the right contacts or should we be engaged with the Field rather than HQ or both? Based on how the team discussions progress, we may make changes and adjust the plan.

If there are real problems with specific relationships, particularly in small businesses, the decision during the Review process maybe to drop the account. That would be an example of radical change. The client could be giving you more headaches than the actual business you're getting. Using the Pareto[16] principle and seeing that if 20% of your clients really provide you with 80% of the revenues, this client might have to go because it's really impacting your organization in a way that the revenues that are connected with this account are not justifying the pain that it's bringing.

In my experience one of the problems with the whole relationship area is that people make decisions about relationships on their own because that's how they do it in everyday life. There is nothing particularly wrong with building relationships in business the way we do socially because that is how we are comfortable, sincere and genuine. That's how we do it socially, in our day-to-day lives, in our marriages, making, in the social clubs, in every way we interact with people.

But when it comes to business relationships, we need to start evaluating these relationships and ensure we are optimizing our company's time and ours because it can have such an enormous impact on the company's performance. Therefore the decision process, for changes and evaluation, should be made on a team basis with everybody involved.

Depending on how big the account is, as a percentage of our company's business, the review process can go right up to the top, even up to the CEO.

---

16 Pareto Principle: (also known as the **80-20 rule**, the **law of the vital few**, and the **principle of factor sparsity**) states that, for many events, roughly 80% of the effects come from 20% of the causes.

It might stop with the President or it may stop at the CMO, but it should go as high as the customer relationship responsibility goes and should never be made by just one key account or one national account manager.

In my experience you will find that if somebody at the top of the organization is more operational or has a financial or engineering background, they will tend to delegate the whole customer area to their account management group and/or marketing group. That is a big mistake. Not only does the organization need to see a commitment to the client from the very top but the client does also.

One of the best proponents of ensuring solid relationships with, in particular, one account was Don Keough[17] who was the President and CEO of the Coca-Cola Company for many years.

He foresaw how important McDonald's was going to be both to market share as well as to what is sometimes termed 'paid sampling'. In other words, even if you sold the product at cost, there would be a huge pay off in getting the product to consumers in a quality form that enhanced their meal experience and led them to further purchases in cans and bottles.

As McDonald's expanded their restaurant's around the globe, they taught consumers that Coca-Cola should be consumed iced cold. Because they ran a very tight and professional operation they took care that their equipment dispensed the beverages at the right temperature and with the right ratio of syrup to water. They cared. They realized that as with the rest of their operation that stringent standards led to a high level of quality and therefore consumer satisfaction, and resulting return visits.

There is still a myth out there that McDonald's were being supplied a different Coke and other products than elsewhere. Not true. They were just better at ensuring the quality was it's best when dispensed. And because of that, consumers learnt that a quality drink could be poured with dispense

---

17 http://en.wikipedia.org/wiki/Donald_Keough

equipment that was as good as bottles and cans and it introduced them to larger drink sizes.

Don Keough recognized very quickly that this would also teach people that Coke should be consumed with food. As a result everywhere he went he met with McDonald's people, ate at their restaurants, and he met with their restaurant crew and senior executives. This sent a clear message within The Coca-Cola Company as to how important McDonald's was and even clearer message to McDonald's that they were valued and respected as an important customer for Coca-Cola. Such was the strong relationship that Don Keough forged with McDonald's; he later went on to serve on the McDonald's Board.

It's really important that senior management is part of the process of meeting clients and sometimes we need to manage this up to ensure it happens. We need our president or CMO to go in and see a client and help them realize how important they are to the whole business that our company represents.

In some cases, such as the Pareto example, we may decide to walk away from the account because our time in turning that account around may be better spent seeking another one, or spending time on an existing one which is potentially far more profitable and easier to deal with. This would obviously need some senior management approval, so typically we would involve as many of management involved in the specific accounts being reviewed, as possible.

If changes are agreed then the *Goals* and *Key Initiatives* need to be changed accordingly. And most importantly, timing needs to be agreed for completion. I've been in meetings where everybody's agreed that a change needs to be made and they walk out of the meeting and everybody's perception is different about when that's going to happen, and in some cases even what was agreed too! That's why the changes need to be recorded.

If we're going to make a change on a relationship or the way an account is being handled, we must allow enough time for that to happen and then measure whether that's actually happening after an amount of time that's reasonable. Relationships take time to build and change.

Measurement

Measurement can take several forms but at its simplest level can be just a calculation of the number of 'reds', 'yellow' and 'green' relationships marked as cells at the start of the process, the base and then how many again at any chosen time.

For example, one account we may have 8 'red', 5 'yellow' and 4 'green' relationship grading's in the first map. At the second quarter review or after 6 months, we look at this again and we may have 5 'red', 5 'yellow' and 7 'green' which shows an obvious improvement. Of course this assumes that some of our 'greens' have not slipped back to 'yellow' or some of the 'yellow' back to 'red' although in some cases that will happen. So it's not a statistically accurate measure, but like most research it indicates a trend.

In Figure 9 you can see a great example of a chart that has been derived from quarterly reviews from within a company CRM system.

Figure 9:

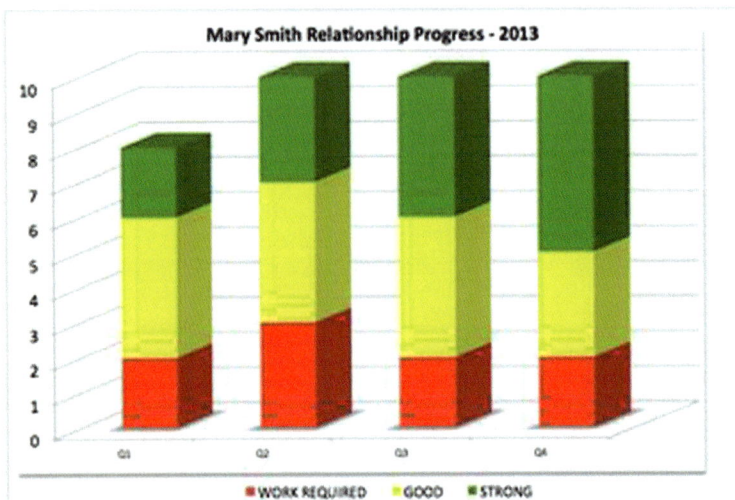

Mary Smith Relationship Progress - 2013

WORK REQUIRED   GOOD   STRONG

If Mary Smith had 8 relationships in quarter one and 2 of them were Weak, 4 of them were Good and 2 were Strong. As a result of the first Quarterly Review, Mary had 10-targeted contacts and at the end of the second quarter we can see she had increased her Strong relationships to 3, Good remained the same and Work Required has increased by 1.

By the end of the year i.e. quarter 4; it was clear she had made progress in achieving her Goals of converting more of her relationships to Strong.

As you can see here, we can track progress over time and that's really the best way to effectively assess progress for people who look after accounts.

Performance Reviews

Relationship Mapping is most successful when you build targets into performance reviews so the measurable aspect has direct input into remuneration. This means that the *Goals* we set and we talked about in the last Chapter, using the traffic light frame of reference of moving from 'red' to 'yellow' or 'yellow' to 'green', are put into the performance appraisals and objectives of those individuals.

If Performance Appraisals are really taken seriously and carried out professionally with due care and attention for employees, then I would suggest building in at least the top three priority Goals into individual Performance Appraisals. This way, there is no doubt that team members are being really measured on their Relationship Goals and if salary increase and bonus are tied to these, then it gets people's attention fairly quickly.

With financial years January to December, business-planning cycles in most companies I've worked with tend to start in July/August and get completed by end October. The Relationship Strategy Plan should be embedded in the same process and be part of the Business Plan and like the Business Plan elements that filter into the Performance Appraisal, so should the Goals from the Account Strategy Plan.

Integration into Business Plans

As I have mentioned earlier, the Relationship Strategy Plan or how we engage better with our customer or client should not be a separate plan just for the account management team. If it is, it is not nearly as powerful as if it is part of the overall company or organizations Business Plan. Last year I spent considerable time with one of my clients devising a template for the Customer or Relationship Strategy Plan so it could be integrated into their company business plan.

One of the things that I've learned over the last few years, and I've written extensive business plans whilst working for Coca-Cola and Philip Morris, is that every major company does a business plan every year and it's normally a two to three year plan. Many companies stopped doing five-year plans for two reasons; senior management realized it was unlikely they would be around in five years anyway and in today's digital world, business circumstances change dramatically quicker.

During the time I was writing the business plans, one of the things I realized is that the business plans never included the people that you deal with to make these things happen. They're great objectives. They're great strategy and they're great tactics, but who the heck is going to do all this stuff and sell it for you at the customer level?

Using an App.

Lastly, to help us with this fast changing world of relationships and to reduce the administrative burden, I have created an App. So we can be quick and flexible and adjust for executive changes or anything that goes on with the account we need to be able to update things digitally rather than having to go back to a spreadsheet. When we agree on changes at the reviews, we can easily record those changes. The App. called *ConnXN Relate* or just *Relate* is available for testing through the

App Store and can be used on Android as well as iOS mobile devices. Web based, all the heavy lifting is done on the web and then quick changes and updates can be undertaken, whilst on the move, with the mobile device. I will help you take a brief look at the App. and it's capabilities in the next Chapter.

This process, I can assure you, delivers an easily understandable, measurable, and efficient plan to ensure the relationship goals are delivered. If followed thoroughly, with regular business reviews, and executed vigorously, it will ensure the Relationship Strategy Plan is accomplished.

SUMMARY

- To ensure we stay on track we need to review and measure progress on a quarterly basis.
- Goals that are built into Performance Reviews have a much higher likelihood of being achieved.
- Using some or all of these three can do the necessary measuring to ensure we really are making improvements in our relationship engagement:
  o Quarterly Reviews
  o Performance Appraisals.
  o Data Measurement by Individual, Team, Company Aggregation.
- **We can measure relationship progress in three ways:**
  o Individually
  o By Account
  o By Company
- There is an App. available that can make building and tracking the relationship roadmap and the Customer Strategy Plan easy and flexible.

ACTION

1. Decide on the review process and how to measure progress.

2. Think who would you want in the quarterly review meetings and what would be the objectives?

3. Who could help you facilitate building the Relationship Strategy Plan into Company Business Plans?

4. Check out the 'ConnXN Relate' App by going to the App Store for iOS devices or Google Play for the Android version. Send me an Email to Peter.Beaumont@ConnXN.net and I will provide you an Email address and Password to allow you access on a test basis.

SIX

USING THE 'RELATE' APP

How to Simplify the Mapping and Planning Process

We have made the whole process of Relationship Mapping and developing the Relationship Strategy Plan really easy. You know, at first we were doing the Mapping and Strategy Planning with Excel and PowerPoint software. But we realized that this was administratively really burdensome, particularly for making any changes that we had to make on a quarterly basis. The Map is a living breathing, evolving thing and as such we need to make it easy to change and update.

So we looked at ways of simplifying the process. Most people now choose an App. over a web search to get to their favorite subject matter. It is a quicker and a more familiar environment. At the WWDC, or Apple Worldwide Developers Conference held in June 2014 in San Francisco, Tim Cook CEO of Apple announced that there are 300,000,000 visitors to the App store very week who can view 1.2 million Apps that are housed there and 75 billion Apps have been downloaded. It appears to be the way to go.

So to help make the Relationship Engagement process more efficient and productive, this seemed the optimum way to go for us too. I developed an App. called ConnXN *Relate* or *Relate* and in this Chapter I will provide you a really brief overview of how it works and then you can try it yourself by going to the App Store or Google Play and downloading it.

It has taken me some to develop this App, but I am now very happy with what it does and the way it is intuitive. Is this the optimum creation and version? No because it will evolve both based on what we learn as well as what we may adapt based on your needs.

There could be several variations out there of the same basic platform. We will constantly tweak the design and function and evolve what it does. However, what I wanted to do in this chapter is give you a feel and look of some of the features.

You will remember that the first step to creating our Relationship Strategy Plan is to *Understand* and map the relationships.

When we first open the App, we have to enter an e-mail address and password and then the landing page is revealed. Here we find a short explanation about the ConnXN *Relate* App and we have a short menu bar, which I'll explain shortly. Here's what the landing page looks like:

Figure 10:

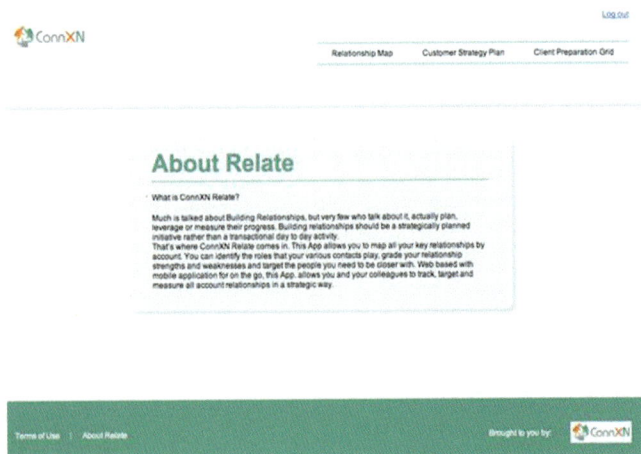

To start using the App. let's imagine that we are going to paint a picture. The Map is our canvas we need to create a background on our canvas before we can start painting our picture.

The background will consist of the names of all our key contacts at the customer and all the names of our company people that *touch* the customer. Let's call our company *ConnXN* (seems like a good name) and our customer *Digital Inc.* So down the y-axis we'll enter the names of our customer contacts and along the x-axis our own company personnel.

Figure 11:

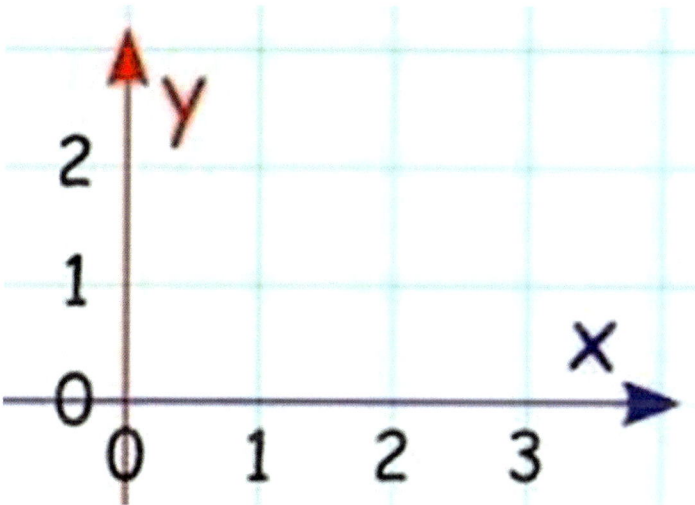

Once we have our background, we can then start to paint our picture and this is accomplished by the use of an easy to find drop down menu that allows us to fill in the various *Decision Influences* by contact as well as grade our relationships, as we explained in Chapter III. As we complete our picture it would start to look a little like this:

Figure 12:

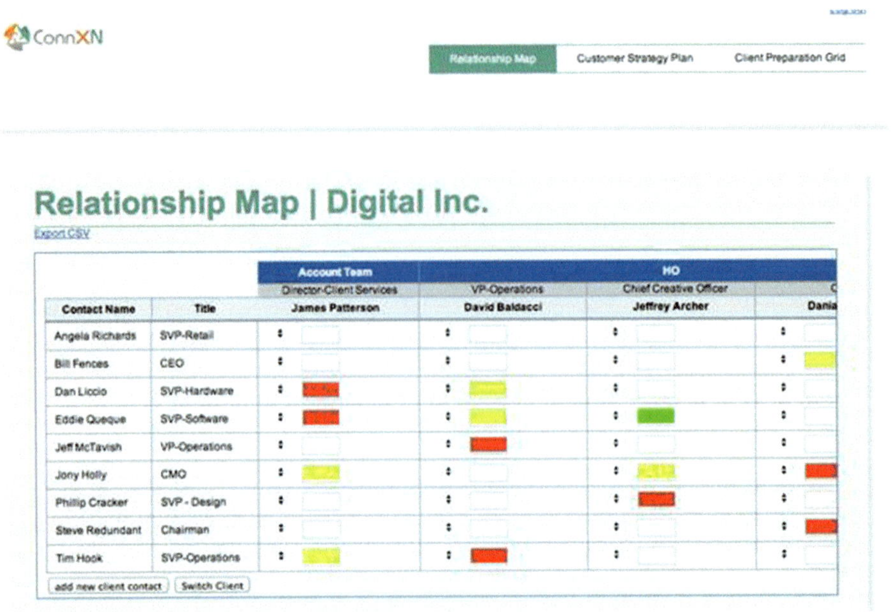

The design is simple to follow, and changing and updating is made easy with various drop down menus.

When the picture looks fairly complete, we need to start thinking about what we are going to do about the issues we can see as explained in Chapter Four, as well as set *Goals* and define our *Key Initiatives*. To do this we move to the second section of the menu bar labeled *Customer Strategy Plan* and on opening this we have an easy to use planning document from where we enter all the information required. We can save, edit and create new versions and they are all archived here:

The last section in the menu bar has not been discussed yet and will be covered briefly in Chapter Ten It is a section called Client Preparation Grid or CPG, and is where we can prepare for upcoming meetings.

Figure 13:

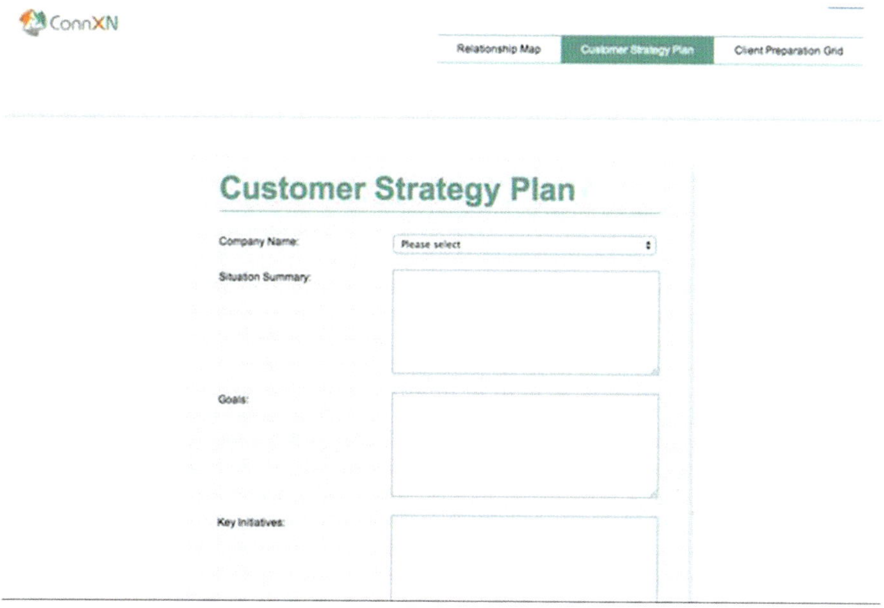

As you can see, the flow of the Apps to a Relationship Strategy Plan follows the Six Steps to a Relationship Strategy plan process. We create our background and then paint our picture based on what we know about our relationships (*Understanding*) and then *Identify* the Customer Influences.

We then review the Map and go to the second section of the menu bar labeled *Customer Strategy Plan* and analyze the situation and list all the *Issues*. Having established our list of Issues, we then decide what we are going to do about them and list them in priority order, as these are our *Goals*.

We then set Key Initiatives so as to ensure the Goals get implemented. And all these steps can be captured in the App.

SUMMARY

- To ensure we can quickly capture the situation and be able to update evolving relationships, we have an easy to use App. called ConnXN *Relate*.
- The App follows the Six Steps to a Relationship Strategy Plan process.
- A free version of the App can be obtained via the App store or Google Play

ACTION

1. Just download the App and try it out.

SEVEN

ESTABLISHING RELATIONSHIPS

Adding value and the effects of technology

"Build lasting relationships by treating others with integrity and giving your full attention when you're with them." - Carey Cavanaugh

Once we have evaluated where we are with relationships, set our *Goals* and *Key Initiatives* we need to decide how we can best improve these relationships. In this Chapter and the next we'll explore ways that we can improve our relationships and raise the bar on the current levels.

So what are the likely effects of not having a good relationship with your customer? I suppose we all had some experience with that, but a good relationship really is a common interest where the customer believes that there is a true win-win potential in the relationship. Therefore, the opposite of that, not having a good relationship, can be indicated in many ways. Not returning calls, not returning emails, not responding to questions are all indicators that mean people are not interested in forming a bond or a business relationship that will eventually end up in some kind of transaction.

Business relationships do not differ from personal relationships because relationships **are** personal. Only **you** can build them and own them. Your company can't; your friends can't. They are yours and only yours. So building relationships in business is much the same as building the ones we develop out of work. We should treat them in the same way.

Relationships start as acquaintances, which are characterized by occasional contacts. At this stage, it is not clear they will lead anywhere. They start by a meeting in the street, at a social event, or by an introduction from another friend.

Similarly, in the work environment they start as an introduction or at a meeting that you attended. We learn people's names and share questions such as "Where are you from?" "Where do you live?", "Do you have kids?", "How many and what ages are they?", "What do you do?".

Acquaintances then progress to Casual Friendships, which can develop quickly, even with initial contacts. The relationship progresses as you mutually discover common interests, activities and concerns. As the relationship evolves so a trust develops and you discover each other's goals, wishes and views. This level has been described as an "oneness of the soul."

Casual friendships normally progress to a Close Friendship and the relationship can then be described as Companions. We can have many Acquaintances and Casual Friendships. However, Companions requires that both persons tend to share the same life goals and these are discussed and become specific in their description. More time is spent together and each person is very comfortable in each other's company. Silence is not quickly filled with words, as it's not necessary.

The last and ultimate level of relationship is becoming Partners. This tends to be an intimate relationship. At this highest level of relationship, both people are prepared to generously invest in one another's lives with the goal of helping each other mature. Friends in this place have the freedom to correct one another and point out each other's blind spots. The personal manifestation of this would of course be marriage. Of course, this level seldom occurs in a business environment. When it has, the results are often mixed and conflict of interest issues are often raised!

So how do we move through these various stages and how do we build relationships? Meaningful relationships are rarely formed across a desk or meeting table. That is too formal and inflexible.

We need to move away from the normal business environment. Make things more personal. If eating out is the preferred first step of moving the environment, dinners and lunches are all very well, but they are still normally in a business environment.

What about lunch or dinner on a boat, on a barge, or at a dinner theatre? Better still is to establish what interests your customer has and then invite him or her to join you in that environment, whether that be a sports, music or other type of entertainment event. This gives you both the opportunity to move from Acquaintance to Casual and/or Companion relationships by enjoying each other's company with something of genuine mutual interest.

Charles Battle[18] was very active in Atlanta's bid to host the Olympic Games in 1996 and is credited with changing the way Olympic Committees hosted and entertained as well as being instrumental in ultimately getting the event to Atlanta. He served as Managing Director for International Relations of the Atlanta Committee and is now working as an International Advisor to the Pyeongchang, South Korea Bid Committee who are seeking to win the right to host the 2018 Olympic Winter Games.

His view on building relationships with the IOC, the International Olympic Committee, was instead of giving them loads of lavish gifts, and

---

18 http://www.millermartin.com/attorneys/charles-h-battle-jr

taking them to lots of great dinners, was to invite them into the hospitality of the southern homes.

When he was pursuing the opportunity for Atlanta to host the Olympics he changed the paradigm on the entertainment of the visiting International Olympic Committee (NOC). Traditionally there would be many elegant, expensive and entertaining events such as dining occasions well as proffered gifts.

He split the groups up in Atlanta and they ended up going into people's homes and experiencing southern hospitality. It changed the whole concept of how the Olympic Committee was entertained and looked after. He apparently said: "You don't need elegant, expensive dinners – invite people into your home." It appears it helped, as although these things are never due to one thing alone, I'm sure it had a major contribution to helping bring the Olympic Games to Atlanta.

Adding Value

Adding value is an expression that is used a lot now, and it can mean a variety of things as it can mean many things to many different people. My interpretation of value is that it is something you add to what someone does to help fulfill their ambition in ways they hadn't considered or hadn't got the resources to do themselves.

The most effective way to build relationships is to bring value to the relationship. This is best achieved by looking at things through the eyes and minds of the customer. What are they trying to achieve and how can you help them in that quest? Even the small things can help.

A few years ago, one of my clients had received an iPad and was taking it out of the box when I entered her office. We quickly chatted about the iPad, as I had owned one for 18 months and I'm very into techy stuff and love my iPad and all Apple products. This was the first time she had owned a tablet and was wondering how to get started.

I had, only that week (timing is everything) come across an article on CNET[19] that cited "25 and 50 tips for the iPad." I suggested I forward the links and she was very enthusiastic. At the end of the meeting, as I left her office I re-iterated that I would send the links and when I forwarded my meeting notes that afternoon after I had returned to my office, from my iPad, which I duly did.

The following day I received a lovely e-mail thanking me profusely for remembering to do it and how much it helped her get up and started on her proud possession that very evening! She said nothing about the meeting notes, but dealt with that in a separate e-mail. It's often the little things that can provide more value, and build trust and respect than many of the more obvious directly related business opportunities.

On of my key contacts when I was working with McDonald's in Vienna Austria was a marketing manager at McDonald's in Prague, Czech Republic. Igor had not been there long and it was fairly obvious he didn't understand how to brief his agency and when I was in a couple of meetings with him the agency was dictating to him what should and shouldn't be done.

He was obviously uncomfortable with that and felt that he wasn't really contributing as much as he should, was losing face and was not in control. A few days later I was in an internal meeting with Coke marketing people and mentioned this situation and asked them if we could help him by unobtrusively having him spend time with our agency that could demonstrate best practices. They agreed they could set something up. I now had to create the opportunity in a way that was non-threatening or indeed not condescending.

So I when I next saw Igor, after some conversation I said: "We've been dealing with our agencies for quite a long time and some of our people have built up a great rapport, which as a result means we have a

---

19 http://www.cnet.com/

really good understanding and therefore get some really good ideas. Over the years we have built a solid process and wondered whether you might want to take a look and apply some of our ideas."

"If you'd like, I am sure I could arrange for us to spend a day over at our agency where they're looking at pitches and stuff like that and I'll take you through the agency and introduce the people. You could then spend a day they're sitting in on meetings and talking to their senior people and see what they do? What do you think?"

He was extremely interested and so I took him to our agency for a day and he quickly learned from the experienced people around how agency meetings took place with clients. He sat in on some really important meetings. As a result of that, he learned some great things about how to work with an agency. We put him in a position where he instinctively picked it up and went away with huge learning's.

I am sure he appreciated what we'd done, although he never formally recognized it. However, the relationship improved dramatically and he was a lot more open and sharing with us than he had previously been.

Another example of adding value concerned McDonald's and consumer marketing back in the 90's. McDonald's was not necessarily consumer concentric about how they did things. They built restaurants, opened them up, and sold hamburgers because they expected people to just flock in and buy them. By the way they did and still do, but things have changed since then and things have got a lot tougher for them, as with others in their industry.

Few people not directly associated with McDonald's, realize that they do not do a lot of the marketing strategy. It's done by their agencies. This is in complete contradiction of the way Coca-Cola operated. Coca-Cola generates their own marketing strategy and brand direction and their agencies facilitate their tactics. Coca-Cola's view is that this is our brand and we will control our own destiny.

Coca-Cola is a marketing company whereas McDonald's is an operations company. One of the things we did at Coke was help McDonald's start dictating their own destiny by understanding and going out and doing focus groups and understanding what the consumers thought about their modus operandi. What was quality like? Did they trust the company? What were the things in the restaurant they liked?

They'd never looked at it that way before. We added a lot of value to the relationship by helping do two things. Teaching them things that didn't sound like we were teaching and secondly, by providing resources that we had.

The Coca-Cola Company started investing millions in market research, instigated when Sergio Zyman[20] was the CMO. He took leadership on understanding the consumer and I remember once sitting in Austria with a group of people that he enthralled telling us stories of a recent trip he'd made to Russia where he sat in people's apartments and listened to consumers talking about their lifestyles and consumption habits. He was very much a pioneer of understanding and listening to consumers.

We made this research available to McDonald's for nothing. Where it made sense, we would meet and present the research to their marketing teams providing incredible consumer insights that saved them thousands of dollars and months of time. This was incredible added value and was yet another way that Coca-Cola raised the level of the relationship from a partner to a strategic partner, more of which we will explore in the next chapter.

A small example of thoughtfulness and providing value is remembering people's birthdays. The most important gatekeepers in any company are the Administrative Assistants. They can get you or prevent you from getting

---

20 http://en.wikipedia.org/wiki/Sergio_Zyman

meetings with key people. They are the unsung heroes. And they know that. Recognize them and respect them.

Ensuring that Administrative Assistants are taken out for occasional lunches and receive flowers on their birthdays are great ways of doing just that. It isn't always lavish presents or social events that build relationships, as Charles Battle demonstrated. It's most often the small things that add value and are the most effective and most remembered.

The agency I worked for understood that and had a standing order for flowers to be delivered to on all the Administrative Assistants that we dealt with, at McDonald's HQ in Oakbrook, Illinois.

When I worked at the agency I would often 'walk the halls'. That is I had an official pass as if I was an employee of the company, and had the freedom of the building. I would often just do a 'walk around' just saying Hi, stopping at peoples cubicles to have a quick chat, but never imposing or preventing people continuing with their work.

I made a point of learning whom sat where and stopping by to share and receive news. News exchanged in this manner was of far more value than reading it an e-mail and because it's not in print, people tend to be much more generous with their news. And by the way, you get the real raw and unedited scoop.

One such 'drop by' revealed to me that the Executive Assistant I was talking too had carelessly lost her Boss. The recently appointed Chief Brand Strategy Officer had moved on and she had no Boss! Sandra was not about to lose her job because of seniority and his role would be replaced, but she was sad! I sent her some flowers to cheer her up, simply that! I received a lovely e-mail thanking me, and thought no more of it.

Several months later we needed to get in and see the EVP for Operations who we had not talked to before and we really needed to see. We had an issue, which needed his approval, and we knew that as he travelled a lot his schedule was going to be packed. I called the assigned number for his Admin and guess who it was? Yep, it was Sandra. She had to been transferred. And guess who got their appointment for the following day?

In providing value, it's important not to confuse this with just merely donating of gifts and trinkets that will hopefully enamor the client. The owner of one of my previous employers treated relationships in such a manner. I am sure she did not see it that way, but providing lavish gifts, especially in an environment where companies Business Conduct Policies prevent one from such action, can backfire.

Gifts and trinkets are not real value. She was however inventive with these gifts. Oil paintings and iPhone cases decorated with photos of their families and Apple TV's were just part of the selection she provided. Such gifts are far more palatable if the relationship is strong to start with and they are coupled with true value building engagement. This was not always the case.

To make matters worse, this poor behavior was multiplied when she dropped relationships as soon as the people were of no more use to her. These actions were perceived as mercenary and manipulative and word quickly got around. I think there is a danger that a planned approach, if not natural, will come over as being false and forced and result in at best no progress and at worst, a strong negative reaction.

Impact of Social Media & Technology on Relationships

As Albert Einstein once observed, **"It has become appallingly obvious that our technology has exceeded our humanity"**.

It's true that in this digital world of voice activated customer service, voice mails, instant messaging and texting and with the plethora of social media, it seems on the one hand that we can follow and get followed, liked and make contacts quicker than ever, but on the other hand never actually speak to anyone, as I observed way back in Chapter One. So although it appears we are better connected, there is sometimes no depth to those contacts and therefore I would argue, no real relationships.

So many people think relationships are about how many people they befriend on LinkedIn or Facebook or indeed exchange emails with. People can hide behind technology. If we are not careful, technology is in danger of destroying our relationships because we can hide behind true feelings as we speed date, propose marriage and have a divorce via text messages.

No one answers his or her phones anymore. How many of us listen to automated message when at home and then listen to whose calling before deciding whether to pick up?

How many times do we use e-mail to make introductions, apologies or suggest meetings rather than make a call? We don't go on a date anymore, let alone blind dates. How risky would that be? Instead, we selectively choose a potential date based on their looks, background, career and aspirations all available on-line. Whatever happened to discovery? The romance of noticing a woman or man across the room, and just imagining who they might be and what they might do. We don't make the time and we want to reduce the risk by Internet or speed dating!

Here's my point with all of this. At the risk of being labeled an old fart, how do you REALLY understand issues, hear and provide genuine empathy, be forced to deal with the situation and get real feedback if you hide behind technology? Pretty soon we won't talk to anyone until we get home from the office in the evening. Even then dialogue is becoming challenging. When I get home, my daughter's world revolves around her iPhone and my son is on his iPad. They don't even know I AM home.

Sure, using technology is easier for all of us, but total reliance and overuse can be the road to total self-absorption, selfishness and reduced opportunities for building REAL relationships. So much of how we communicate is body language and so do yourself a favor and just pick up the damn phone, go and talk to someone, take some risks. Who knows, you may discover fun again!

Take people out to social events, as we talked about earlier. Take them away from a desk or a voicemail and sit them in an environment where we can actually get to know each other. Yes, we can make relationships more personal, but it's a bigger effort and sometimes we should to do it because the stakes are worth it.

E-mail and Relationships

E-mail: **"It's not a replacement for the phone, it's not a means to get in touch with someone immediately. Yet the expectation is that it is – or should be."** – Mike Vardy

According to The Radicati Group[21] in 2013 there were 3.9 billion worldwide e-mail accounts, of which 24% were business accounts. That means the number of e-mail accounts exceeds 50% of the worlds population. More data in their research unearths that daily e-mail traffic, i.e. e-mails sent and received was 183 billion, the majority of which, 55% is business traffic. That is a lot of e-mail traffic and probably explains why we all struggle to keep on top of our inboxes. And according to Commtouch's Internet Threats Trend Report[22] in the first quarter of 2013, an average of nearly 100 billion spam e-mails were sent each day. So 55% of our e-mail traffic is spam!

However, are we over using e-mail? Are we using it for the right things? As I said earlier, we now book a telephone call via e-mail! We agree on a date for a call and then formally invite one another so it's on the calendar! Spontaneity, humor and excitement are slowly being strangled by our reliance on e-mail. E-mail is efficient – possibly. Personal? – Not really!

---

21 http://www.radicati.com/wp/wp-content/uploads/2013/04/
Email-Statistics-Report-2013-2017-Executive-Summary.pdf
22 http://www.cyren.com/newsroom.html

Do we use e-mail to avoid conflict? Do we use it to avoid feeling uncomfortable, to overcome shyness, inferiority complexes, doubts, apprehensions, and any manner of other psychological and emotional problems? It's our version of the massive proliferation of vending machines you find in Japan, where choice and interaction with machines is preferred to exchanges with people. We use it to overcome our fear of selling, to make sure we're never caught off guard or put on the spot. We have convinced ourselves that this is all more advanced, more efficient, and more productive.

But, what about the missed opportunities and unnecessary misunderstandings that come when we use e-mail instead of phone calls?

Now, I don't live in a cave in fact, far from it. I also have joined the great technological and digital arena. I have always been a gadget geek! Our household of 2 adults and 2 kids aged 11 and 14, possesses 2 MacBook Airs, 4 iPhones, 3 iPad's, a 27" iMac and 3 iPod's. I have 6 e-mail accounts and deal with the same proliferation of real and junk mail that everyone else does everyday! And I therefore face the same dilemmas that I am observing.

These tools are replacing face-to-face communication. And here lies the human disconnect. At the very least, we need to hear someone's voice (even if it's just on the phone). E-mail seldom works when conflict needs to be resolved: We often say things via e-mail we would not say if we were not safely behind the screen. There are several reasons that communicating through conflict should occur in person; or at the very least by telephone, but never via e-mail. Lastly, e-mail is not effective for communicating private or proprietary information: e-mail is far from being private, as Edward Snowden has famously demonstrated.

In order to maintain a healthy relationship, people need to express themselves openly and honestly. This means that each person is able to express positive feelings, negative feelings, complaints, desires, and needs.

This is always done best verbally! However, verbal communication is only effective when both or all parties are effective listeners. Listening doesn't simply mean hearing. It necessitates understanding another person's point of view. Because we have so many e-mails and try to multi-task while doing them, we seldom really read all of them. If we do, we don't fully comprehend them. We are becoming a twitter generation where we only read 140 letters, equivalent to 30 words, at a time. Anything longer than a short paragraph is skipped.

E-mail is another of our communication devices that I belief can hinder not help the building of relationships.

When it matters, make it personal. Take the time to make a call or visit personally. It will make an enormous difference to the way your message is received and understood and reacted too.

Embedding

Another way of getting close, is being embedded in the company's offices.

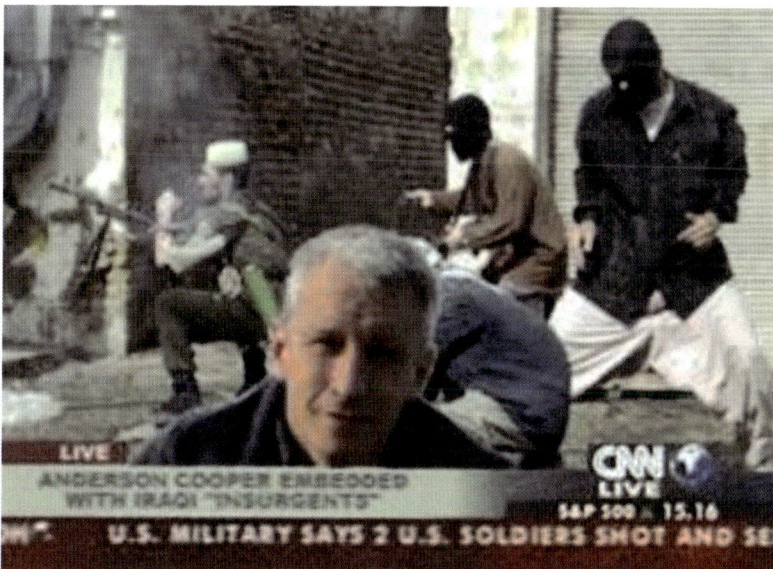

This expression became popular when CNN started using it when referring to one of their reporters being placed in the battlefield in Iraq, bringing real time reports of combat. Many years ago, while I was with Coca-Cola in the UK, one of my senior managers charged me with getting closer to Beecham Foods (as they were known then) who was our distributor in the grocery trade. Left to their own devices for many years, Beecham Foods was using Coca-Cola as door openers for their own brands on which they made better margins.

I was charged with taking leadership and getting more allegiance for our brands. I needed to understand their business first. So I virtually camped out there. Without being a nuisance I would book meetings with people to learn their business, and between the meetings be in the cafeteria, in corridors and just hang out asking questions and taking notes. After 6 months the head office provided me a desk and my own extension number.

Nearly 30 years later I was working for Creata, and I was once again embedded by being provided an office space in the McDonald's Global Corporate HQ offices in Oak Brook, Illinois. This ultimate engagement means you are seen as an extension of your client's business.

You are invited to meetings you would never normally be part of and you have easy access to people and resources providing numerous opportunities to provide real value and build trust and respect for you and your company. But the real benefit in being embedded is that you get to understand your customers' business and look through their eyes at their objectives and the challenges they face everyday.

So there are various ways to build better relationships and in the next Chapter we will move on and look at how to solve relationship issues.

SUMMARY

- Building business relationships is personal and needs to be treated in that manner. Only you can build them and own them.
- To build meaningful relationships we often need to move away from the normal business environment.
- Value is something you add to what someone does to help fulfill their ambition in ways they hadn't considered or hadn't got the resources to do themselves.
- Look for ways you can add value to help your customers.
- Don't let technology get in the way of building genuine personal relationships.

ACTION

1. Jot down the names of the key relationships you have identified that you need to improve, and make notes of some of the ways you can build a better relationship.
2. Using the same list, identify the primary interests of those same people and think of events they would really like to attend.
3. Using your notes integrate them into your Key Initiatives in your Relationship Strategy Plan as ways of achieving your Goals.

EIGHT

BUILDING BETTER RELATIONSHIPS

Dealing with Difficult Situations

In my experience, the majority of business issues can be solved amicably when a good relationship exists, as it allows a mutual understanding of each other's point of view so that any negotiations become a conversational discussion rather than a heated competitive debate.

Having good relationships allows flexibility and a preparedness to give and take.

I would maintain that whether you sell products, solutions or ideas, you still are selling a service. In other words, you are suggesting something that will add value or enhance something they already have or are trying to accomplish. Therefore, it is key that that we understand the Customers Notion and that if we have relationships that are not as good as they should be that we take steps to improve them.

Having a mutual understanding through good relationships can help us in difficult situations. In fact a good relationship helped me overcome a very difficult situation, which was leading towards a rift with the Coca-Cola and McDonald's relationship as well as potential damage to my credibility and personal career.

During the time I worked for Coca-Cola, I enjoyed a role for 10 years on the McDonald's business. That is to say I was responsible for our business with Coca-Cola's Number One customer in Europe, Middle East, Africa and India. I had a ball. It was probably the best job I ever had. I worked with great customers, fantastic colleagues and super management on one of the best brands in the world, serving one of the best brands in the world and travelled in one of the most exciting areas in the world!

With over 30 countries to coordinate you can probably imagine when I woke up I sometimes had problems remembering which country I was in, let alone what time it was! Obviously my prime role was to increase sales of Coca-Cola and other brands, such as Fanta, Diet Coke and Sprite through McDonald's restaurants.

But I was also charged with policing our pricing arrangement, which was at times complicated and had a number of exceptions built in for countries with high inflation and unstable currencies.

On a global basis, I seemed to have most of those exceptions. For example, in Poland the monthly inflation rate in January 1990, was 80%, and in 1994 the Russian Ruble exchange rate to the $US dollar was 63,379 Rubles to one US Dollar compared to the 30 it is today. This created a lot of headaches for our centrally formed pricing protocol.

Eastern Europe was struggling to come to terms with their identities, as their frequent peep shows behind the iron curtain had now become full frontal nudity as the curtain disappeared forever. This meant they now had to face the uncomfortable economic and social decisions of how to develop and therefore we saw these struggling currencies with inflation and rising prices. Factors like this made any kind of coordinated pricing strategy extremely difficult.

One of my key relationships was the person who headed up the McDonald's Supply Chain (or Purchasing or Buyer) for Central Europe. (To protect and respect the various people that are part of the real situations I describe throughout the book, most of the time I have not used their real names).

Based in Vienna, and born in former Yugoslavia, Gorin's role was to develop a supply chain across this new un-curtained area, whilst the political and economic climate changed like the shifting sands of the Gobi desert. This meant his role was developing beef, chicken, cheese, potatoes and other key food suppliers to the highest levels that McDonald's demanded in an area that lacked any great agriculture expertise. He wanted the very highest quality at the lowest price and he did not take prisoners if he did not get what he wanted.

Gorin was very good at what he did, but he could become vindictive. Unfortunately for me, I became one his targets. He was not happy with our pricing and so in one of his vindictive spasms he sent an e-mail to a number of senior people in both Coca-Cola and McDonald's that in essence blamed me for not being a good partner and facilitating better prices.

He decided that one of the ways to do this was to expose me within my organization and his organization as being uncooperative. I had tried to get on with this guy in every way possible. I even took him off to play golf. I hired a professional at our nearby Golf course to coach us both so we could get closer but it didn't appear to be getting me anywhere. My golf however, <u>was</u> improving.

I was appalled. He had not discussed this with me prior to sending the e-mail and any response to all those copied would look like a defensive one by me. I had worked for over 5 years with Gorin and we had worked diligently through pricing as well as helping McDonald's in a number of markets to get local supplies for them where our bottlers, who were already there and had established contacts and supply arrangements, and could introduce them to their network.

In one such case in Russia, we had supplied McDonalds' sugar from our bottling plant to help them out until their supplies cleared the bureaucratic customs process in Moscow.

I felt betrayed. I put my heart and soul into servicing this customer and I felt like a condemned man that had now been thrown into a Roman amphitheater to face the gladiator! I agonized for days about what to do. I discussed with my boss the cause and implications.

Finally I decided to take it head on. As I said earlier, the cornerstone of meaningful relationships are trust and respect and I felt that Gorin and I had built this over the years and he had betrayed the trust by just throwing me to the wolves for his own personal gain because I wouldn't give him what he wanted.

We had a pricing meeting scheduled which would consist of 6 people, including us, at the McDonald's HQ for Eastern Europe which was located at Vienna airport. I arrived early and he came out of his office to see me and I asked him whether we could have 5-10 minutes alone before the meeting.

I had decided I had only one card really left to play, which was to confront the issue. But I had to be delicate. I didn't give him any warning, but said, "I'd appreciate it if you and I could have 10 minutes together before the meeting starts. Is that OK?" He said, "Sure."

So we proceeded into his office and he closed the door and we sat down, traded comments about the weather a few jokes and then I said to him "Gorin, I'm really concerned with the e-mail you sent last week. I felt that over the last 5 years I had demonstrated both my commitment to

McDonald's as well as personal respect for what you are trying to do and that we had a high element of mutual trust. I love what I do and I love McDonald's as a customer and I've always put you first when I've been able to do so. I personally have tried to add value in everything we do with McDonald's and have even helped you open up new markets with our resources, which has allowed you to fast track your expansion plans.

I've helped your team by sharing a lot of our market research and opened our books to things like the business planning process we use. Therefore, I'd like you to understand what effect that e-mail has had on me. It has demotivated me and I feel it was unfair. It makes me feel undervalued, that you don't respect me and that frankly you think I'm not doing my job. Unfortunately that's how I believe the others you copied will see it too. It puts me in a very difficult position with my role now and in the future. Can I ask you why you thought it was necessary to do this and what we can do to fix things, if in fact you want to."

It was very interesting. He backpedaled for about 20 minutes. I couldn't even get a word in. He suddenly realized he'd hit a sensitive part of me and, by the way, I realized I'd done the same. His reaction was astounding.

Gorin took pains for over 20 minutes to explain this was not the desired effect he anticipated from the e-mail, that he did trust and respect what I did for him and his company and that his e-mail was really directed at both our senior management to fix some of the issues we had been struggling with.

At the end of our one on one meeting, we ended up very amicably understanding each other's point of view. So much so that later, Gorin sent out a clarifying e-mail, which exonerated me and pointed the blame for the pricing situation at our senior management.

But this meeting could never have taken place with that result if I had not spent the time and invested in building that trust and respect over the years. So, I believe good customer relationships are THE key to a successful business.

Different Strokes for Different Folks

A question I have often been asked is whether building relationships is one size fits all? Is there a different strategy for building relationships with senior management versus junior management?

My answer has been that building relationships tends to be the same whoever it is. It's some and all of the things I have been discussing up to now. Find the common ground, add value and connect on a personal level, as well change the environment.

Where the differences will be, of course, depends on the **their** goals, aspirations and lifestyles. The other thing that will be different is access to the person you seek a relationship with. The more senior the person is, the more likely it is that people will protect their time and access to that person. Both they and others will limit their time available outside of their crammed schedules.

You have to be cognizant of the fact you're not going to get a CEO to accept a luncheon appointment if you're fairly middle level executive. So, what do you do about it if that's really important? What you do is enlist your own CEO or CMO to arrange it. Suddenly, that's attractive because they're of the same level and you will more likely get that luncheon appointment than if you reached out to do it yourself. Maybe that relationship that we talked about earlier, with the all-powerful, all-seeing Administrative Assistant can help you get that meeting.

Communications will also differ for different levels of management. If you are looking to invite a CEO for lunch, you may want to write e-mail and then maybe follow up by phone. But if it's a junior manager, you might want to text, instant message or leave a voice mail.

Finding the Common Ground

I'm a great believer in moving relationships from behind a desk to a more common and informal ground. It may be a social event or sports event where you can ask the kind of questions that you would do of a friend. Friendship develops when you can understand more about what makes that guy or lady tick. When you start to discuss their interests and find the mutual ones and show each other pictures on your phone, there's a good indicator that you are getting connected.

One of the things that was impressed on us when I was in training at Cadbury's was to always look after the guy on the back door at the Tesco supermarket chain because he could well be the Manager next week. And this was often the case.

This psychology follows the lines of being nice to the people on your way up as you may meet them again on your way down. Back in the 1970's Tesco was growing rapidly and goals and targets were tough and lack of reaching them resulted in high Manager turnover, much like what happens to NFL and Premier League soccer coaches nowadays. There is very little patience for poor results. So the lesson then and is as sound now, is have relationships up and down an organization and treat everyone well. You never know whom you could be dealing with next.

One of the things that I think is really interesting is the cultural difference in the way relationships are formed. As I pointed out, from David Nour's excellent observations in Chapter One, in the US business tends to come first and relationship second. As the pace of life tends to be much quicker in the US than most other countries, so most business is discussed first and then the relationship may develop afterwards. In Europe and Asia the relationships tend to come first and the business develops from the forming and growing of those relationships. I think it depends where you come from as to how relationships develop but in today's world with so many different nationalities occupying positions all over the world; it's as well to understand these differences.

However and whenever the relationships are developed my view is that they should not be mercenary or manipulative. They should be genuine, caring and mutual. They should be based on what the other person is looking to get out of their career and their life and matching these as close as possible.

Early on in my position as Vice President for Coca-Cola on the McDonalds business, I had a real challenge to get to know the head of the McDonald's business. Hans (not his real name) was an aggressive leader, with a very direct approach. He had zero toleration for fool's policy and was cavalier in many ways, including his numerous relationships with the female fraternity.

Good looking, and a smart dresser, he was difficult to approach and he surrounded himself with a small and trusted team. He ran his fiefdom HIS way. In corporations this can work…whilst you're successful. The moment you don't deliver the knives come out and all the people you've upset start baying for blood! This was still in the stars for Hans, but right now, he was successful, and very difficult to get too.

One of the things I found out about Hans was that he had taken up golf. At that time many of the senior executive team at McDonald's in Oakbrook, IL played golf. Jim Skinner[23], for example, destined to be the CEO of McDonalds, had a 14 handicap. Hans saw his own internal relationship building opportunity in learning to play golf.

He joined one of the best Golf Clubs on the edge of Vienna, the Colony Club Gutenhof, near Himberg. Extremely competitive, he wanted to be the best immediately. As someone who plays golf and has attempted to master it for many years, I can testify that golf is a game that few people

---

23 http://en.wikipedia.org/wiki/Jim_Skinner

ever master and especially quickly. But here was an opportunity for me to also start playing and engage with Hans.

The thing about a leader wanting to take up a new sport is that his team suddenly wants to do the same thing, but how do they do this without it being too obvious? Yep, I smelt an opportunity here.

About an hour drive (70 miles) south of Vienna was a David Leadbetter golf academy at bad Tatzmannnsdorf, the first one in Europe. I organized a weekend at the resort for a few of Han's team and myself and arranged golf lessons as well as a game on Sunday morning with prizes awarded at lunch before everyone departed. Everyone got a prize for something. It was a great success. We all learnt a lot, improved greatly and it became the basis for a few more of these weekends and events as well and the building of great relationships.

One of the biggest benefits of engaging with Hans, and us becoming friends is that it taught me that if you can engage with the leader, then it becomes a lot easier to engage with his team. It suddenly opens doors that were previously closed and indeed sometimes locked. It's a lot more difficult going the other way! If you are seen in the company of the revered leader, and on obviously good terms, the leaders team sees that engaging with you becomes an opportunity for you to put in a good word for them and get closer to the Boss.

Of course golf was not the only way I established stronger relationships with Hans and his team. I coordinated joint Business Planning meetings between Coca-Cola and McDonald's, marketing input sessions and top-to-top management dinners for example, as ways of further in-depth engagement.

SUMMARY

- Most business issues can be solved amicably when a good relationship exists.

- Good relationships allow a mutual understanding of each other's point of view so that any negotiations become a conversational discussion rather than a heated competitive debate.
- Having good relationships allows flexibility and a preparedness to give and take.
- Be prepared to have the difficult discussion when things get tough.
- Always look for the common ground of interests.

ACTION

1. Study your Relationship Map and identify those contacts that are likely to be the most difficult.
2. List some ways you would handle the difficult situations, by person, to suit their differing characteristics.

NINE

DEVELOPING RELATIONSHIPS

...By Understanding, Asking Questions and Listening

Understanding

"**Before you satisfy 'the client' understand and satisfy the person.**" – Harry Beckwith

So how do we develop a relationship? What are some of the things that we need to do? My view on this is that it all starts with what your customer wants. So many times I've come across people that go in to see customers and all they're interested in is getting them to agree to buy their product, service or idea. They either want to sell them or get them to agree to something, and they may be the same thing. One of the things that resonated with me and I found so helpful in my Account Management roles over the years, was 'Conceptual Selling' by Miller Heiman.[24]

---

24 http://www.millerheiman.com/

Whist I was with Coca-Cola I was fortunate enough to have a particularly enlightened boss who intuitively understood that interpersonal skills were at the heart of sound and effective account management. Rick Nicholas was a student and proponent of Stephen Covey and introduced us to Covey's best-known book *The Seven Habits of Highly Effective People25*. If you have not come across it, Covey's major premise in the book is that values govern people's behavior, but principles ultimately determine the consequences. It has sold more than 25 million copies worldwide since its first publication in 1989.

In addition, Rick introduced us to *Conceptual Selling*. The boiled down concept of 'Conceptual Selling' is that it starts with what **the customer or client** wants instead of what <u>we</u> want. I think until you get inside the head of the person that you're dealing with, you really don't understand how to match your product, service, or idea with what will help them satisfy some need or indeed help them advance in their current job or career.

When you've understood that, then you have the secret formula to success, which is what is the win-win. I think that's how you develop a relationship. You understand what is in their heads and what they want to do. By the way, it's not always just about business. It's often personal.

What are their personal ambitions? Where do they want their career to go? Where do they go on vacation? How many kids have they? What do they do at the weekends? I call all this understanding of the Customer or Clients need and wants, the **Clients Notion.** The Merriam-Webster Dictionary definition of Notion is "an individual's conception or impression of something known, experienced, or imagined (2): an inclusive general concept (3): a theory or belief held by a person or group.

The *Clients Notion* is really to help us understand the individuals we are dealing with as people and what makes them tick. Here are some brief

---

25 http://en.wikipedia.org/wiki/The_Seven_Habits_of_Highly_Effective_
People

examples of three Client Notions that I have extracted from some recent work on this, with names changed.

Mike Burke - Settling in to the CMO role as an outsider. Needs to gain trust of employees. Is cautious not to rock the boat too much. Is ambitious and wants to get some quick wins to impress management. Is new to the country and has few friends.

Karyn Fuu - Feels squeezed between new CMO who wants a global campaign and Asia country managers who have full budget autonomy and divergent marketing tastes and want local control. She has been working in the same role for over 10 years and does not tolerate fools gladly. Her mother is dying of cancer and she spends more time at work to avoid the emotional pain.

Andy Murphy - Has helped lead the global campaign charge but worried that sales figures aren't justifying the approach. Enjoying success at Trident and we have a close relationship with him. Andy is very socially connected, outside of work helps to drive awareness of a disease his son has. Goes on sports weekend with buddies. Involved with the local church.

We all think we probably know our client's business. After all, we have been talking to them for quite a while and they are a well-known name! So what else do I need to know?

If we really want to understand the Customer, their Notion and what they are trying to achieve, we need to know their business; not just by looking at their website, but by understanding how their business works from soup to nuts. We need to know what's involved from supply chain to delivery, their objectives, and how they measure success. It's not always just revenue and profit! Many companies have a sophisticated balanced scorecard approach, wherein lies the secrets of how we could add value to their business.

So how do we get closer to understanding their company? Asking the right questions often provides a lot of the answers. But to get to those questions, we need to understand a little about the business.

Good sources are easy to find, and yes, the Company annual report is a good start. But what are we looking for? Who do we meet and what are their role, background, and experience? What's the revenue, stock, profit situation? Who do you know that knows them? What appears to be their challenges? Sources are existing connections, as well as LinkedIn, web browsers, Wiki, Glassdoor, Hoovers etc.

The word *Partnering* is used a lot now. As with many words, such as *awesome, literally and hot,* when used a lot the words become popular and are then often misused. **True partnering with clients means positioning yourself as an extension of their company and looking for ways to add value to that company, as well as to individuals.**

The only way you can truly partner is to understand our potential partners business and their situation. We need what I call the **Ultimate Engagement**. Ultimate Engagement is 'walking the partners' talk based on actually spending time in their shoes. This means either working in the company's premises or operations.

I am sure you have heard of and probably seen the TV series Undercover Boss. In this program, a company boss works incognito somewhere in his or her company to find out what works and what doesn't. We need to do the same, but without the undercover part. We are less of a threat in working in the Partner's warehouse or in their restaurant, if we are not part of the company. But we can find out a lot about their challenges.

During part of my career working on the McDonald's business with Coca-Cola, we used to work in a McDonald's restaurant several times a year. Wow! What perspective that offered. I learned how the crew was fanatic about quality, focused on service and how fastidious they are about cleanliness. I grilled nuggets, assembled ingredients for Big Macs and found out how extra pairs of hands miraculously appeared from nowhere to help pull the fries when the buzzers told me that several fryers were all ready at the same time.

So what if the people you identify don't want a relationship? Sometimes the chemistry between two people just isn't conducive to producing a relationship. Sometimes you just have to accept that. The way that I've dealt with that in my career, and it's only happened on a couple of occasions fortunately for me, has been to use a third party.

That means even though we should own the primary relationship we 'loan' that role to somebody else for a temporary period to allow us to forge an understanding and build the relationship. I'll give you an example.

I had just been promoted at Creata to be responsible for Client Services for N. America for McDonald's having moved to the US from Europe 3 years previously. Creata is one of two below the line agencies servicing McDonald's and primarily manufacture about 40% of the Happy Meal toys for McDonald's globally. Anyone who thinks that because Brits and Americans speak English means they are culturally the same need to think differently. There is a quote often attributed to Winston Churchill, which sums up differences when he is purported to have famously said, "Britain and America are two nations divided by a common language".

Translated into business implications, this means that although the language may be the same, the cultural differences sometimes means it takes longer for relationships to be formed. When I took on the new role, one of my senior contacts was a Director of Marketing at McDonald's. Kim, not her real name, had been in her role for over 10 years and was experienced and knew the people at our agency very well. I was the new guy on the block, and we needed to ensure we had a good, solid relationship with her. She was aware I had senior Global contacts but I had not really had much to do with the US.

Early meetings indicated that the relationship was going to take a while to develop, as they all do, and I needed trust and respect to be established quickly as we had some challenges with some of the work we were doing on the digital side of the business. In my Department, I had a very good agency person who had worked for McDonald's previously and for our agency for about 10 years and knew Kim quite well. They had worked on several projects together and Annie, again not the real name, had 'grown up' with Kim.

I discussed the problem with Annie and we agreed that she would take the 'lead' on the daily contact and I would gradually build rapport with Kim at larger meetings and events over time. I planned to delegate the relationship to the person who reported to me. I said to Annie, "I just can't make this work as quickly as it needs to and we need to stay close to Kim and ensure we are delivering what she requires." She said, "I'm sure you'll establish a relationship very quickly as you have with others." I said, "No, it's not going to happen. I just feel it. I'm going to make you the owner of that relationship, at least for a limited time but we're not going to make that public. I just want you to own that relationship and bring me in gradually as we see fit."

Annie agreed to play her role and saw the importance of it and it became an effective relationship strategy. After 3 months of being bought into several meetings I was able to start having strategic meetings with Kim and when there were issues, she started calling me more often. Sometimes, we have to accept that somebody else can probably have a better relationship than you, maybe just on a short term basis and therefore, turn it to your advantage and manage it.

Asking Questions

"Ask the right questions if you're going to find the right answers."
- Vanessa Redgrave

So apart from listening what else can we do to better develop our relationships? To understand our customers better we need to ask questions. Not just any questions, but questions that will help us understand more about the person we are talking too and move us forward towards achieving our objectives.

We need to explore the areas that will give you clues as to what that person wants, what they're looking for and what success looks like to <u>them</u>.

To help us think about questions and what we should be asking and why, let's explore a process for this and categorize the type of questions we might ask. I would maintain that there are 4 types of questions and we'll look at each of these briefly and explain what they are and how to use them.

The first is *Confirmation Questions*. These are used to validate data and reveal discrepancies. Whatever answers you get to Confirmation Questions they will always give you more up to date information than you could possibly have if you didn't ask. They are used early in the meeting to makes sure nothing has changed since the last meeting or there is agreement on the purpose of the meeting. You may even want to do both at the same time. Here's an example.

"So John, last time we met we agreed we would run the promotion in July and we would focus on the diet range. Is that still your understanding of where we are and what we'll discuss today?"

The second type of question is *New Information Questions*. These are used, when in our pre-meeting planning (more of this in Chapter Ten), we identify that we need more information of a specific nature to help us understand the customer's situation. This maybe data, location of a plant, timing or when a decision may be made. They tend to use the 4 w's and the h approach i.e. who, what, when, where and how.

Here's another example; "Tell me, if we were to incorporate the regular brands with the diets in the offer, would that change the timing for the promotion?"

The third type is *Attitude Questions*. This is where we focus on the customers gut feel. How they personally feel about what we are suggesting, rather than the results. Normally such questions will reveal the personal information that the customer feels or thinks and will help build a picture of the Customers Notion that we discussed earlier. The main reason for using attitude questions is to reveal what the customer's mental picture is of what success looks like and if they agree with your point of view. We want to find out what they think and certainly not challenge their view. By the way, we can use these types of questions to ask the customer about the personal feelings of other people in their company as well.

An example of an Attitude Question could be; "John, at this point how do you feel about the project and the promotion? What's your opinion?"

And the fourth and last type is *Commitment Questions*. As it implies, these types of questions are meant to get some form of commitment. However, they are not, as some assume, a way of *closing the sale* as some old sales techniques used to call *getting the order*! They are more to tell us at what level we have reached in the process of getting agreement. What still needs to be done to complete a full agreement and what sorts of timing of events are still required to be planned. They are most often used towards the end of the meeting, as it will help us summarize where we are and what action is required for next steps.

An example of a *Commitment Question* could be; "OK, so from what I'm hearing, you agree we can run a promotion on regular and diet brands and still stick to the July timing. Can I go ahead and confirm that to my management?"

So, there's a range of questions we can use as tools to help us both move the conversation along and identify where we are in the process of reaching an agreement as well as developing the relationship. We will look more at the use of these with our App in the next Chapter.

Listening

"You Cannot Truly Listen To Anyone And Do Anything Else At The Same Time." - M. Scott Peck

Listening is such a passive action but most of us just don't do it!

If we are not driving, we are sleeping, and if we are at work we are texting, e- mailing and talking…but rarely listening and I mean really listening. Listening means completely and utterly listening! Not thinking of tonight's activity, the To Do list and the growing e-mail inbox!!

Recent studies have shown that we typically remember only 25-30% of what we hear. However, 'Active Listening' can increase that enormously. One of the ways to practice 'Active Listening' is to remember that eyes and ears should be used in the same proportion they have been allocated. In today's digital world we seem to be continually playing catch up with voice mails, e-mails, meetings and ever increasing tight deadlines. Our kids tend to be watching TV, texting their friends and doing their homework! How do they do that? Well the answer is that they can't all do all those things well at the same time:

So, is it that important? Yes it is. If we don't truly listen we do not get the real message being communicated. It's especially important if we have taken the time to think about the sort of questions we just reviewed and have them prepared, deliver them and then not listen to the reply.

So much of the spoken word is hidden in inflection, tone and expression. If we really want to build relationships and understand what I call the *Customer's Notion*, then we have to become really Active Listeners.

Good listening has to be worked at, and here are some things that I try to adhere too: First: give my full attention to the person who is speaking. I don't look out of the window or at what else is going on in the room. Customers want to see and believe we are interested in what they think, feel and want.

Second: I make sure my mind is focused, too. It can be easy to let our minds wander if we think we know what the client is going to say next, but we might be wrong! If we feel our mind wandering, I change the position of my body and try to concentrate on the speaker's words.

How many times have we been in a situation when we see that the speaker has not been allowed to finish before the other person begins to talk? Speakers appreciate having the chance to say everything they would like to say without being interrupted. Don't we all! When you interrupt, it looks like we aren't listening, even if we really are.

Let ourselves finish listening before we begin to speak! We can't really listen if we are busy thinking about what we want say next. Worse still, I have seen many people jump in and interrupt and finish the sentence for the speaker so they can talk! Not smart. This can only result in hurting the customer's feelings and risking a negative feeling towards us and our manners, or lack thereof!

Listen for main ideas. The main ideas are the most important points the speaker wants to get across. They may be mentioned at the start or end of a talk and repeated a number of times. Pay special attention to statements that begin with phrases such as "My point is…" or "The thing to remember is…"

Asking questions is key to ensuring we have fully understood what the speaker has said. A good technique can often be to play back to the client what we think they said so we can be sure our understanding is correct. For example, we might say, "When you said that that the packaging was not what you were looking for, did you mean it was the color or the shape that was a problem?"

Provide feedback. Body language communicates a great deal, so lounging back sends a message of zero interest and apathy. Now and then, nod to show that we understand. At appropriate points, we may also smile, frown, laugh, or be silent. These are all ways to let the speaker know that we are really listening. Remember, we listen with our face as well as our ears!

It's important to recognize some of these reasons for poor listening. There can be many such as interruptions, perceived failed expectations, preoccupation with something else, or the use of automatic gestures.

A study in Texas (Metcalfe 1997) showed that people remember: 10 percent of what they read, 20 percent of what they hear, 30 percent of what they see, 50 percent of what they see and hear, 70 percent of what they say, and 90 percent of what they do and say. So, when in conversation, be sure to do everything you can to make sure you are being an Active Listener. It also helps explain why I believe that solid, lasting relationships are best built in person and not via digital technology.

Lastly, on the subject of listening, one of my favorite quotes is "You were born with two ears and one mouth for a reason." It originated around 55 AD from Epictetus, the Greek Sage and Stoic philosopher. In case you don't remember what is on the other side of the comma as to why … "so that we can listen twice as much as we speak." If only we practiced the power of this quote.

SUMMARY
- Developing relationships starts with understanding the customer and their needs and aspirations.
- We must be able to define the Customers Notion, which will be personal.
- Asking the right questions in the correct sequence and listening intently will help us better understand the customer as well as help us better develop our relationships.

ACTION
1. Think of the people you meet at the customer now and pick three.
2. Write down what you know about their *Customers Notion*. What do you know about their personal goals, lifestyle and aspirations?
3. If you know very little, plan to ask some attitude questions next time you meet to reveal to you more about THEM. List the questions.

TEN

PREPARING FOR MEETINGS

I f you have got this far, and have read all the Chapters, well done. You should now know pretty much all there is to know about building, maintaining and measuring the right relationships.

Now that we have mapped our relationships, analyzed them, identified the Issues, set ourselves *Goals* and established *Key Initiative*s to accomplish the *Goals*, as well as learnt more about establishing and building better relationships, it's time to think about how we can better prepare for meetings so can achieve our *Goals*.

Any meeting is an opportunity for us to establish better relationships, and in this final chapter we will explore how we can better prepare for meetings so that we can build on our plan.

Earlier, in Chapter Six we looked at the ConnXN App and how it helps us establish and update our Maps as well as capture our Customer or Relationship Strategy Plan (CSP). In that Chapter I referred to a third section on the menu bar of the App., which was the *Client Preparation Grid (CPG)*.

Figure 14:

Relationship Map	Customer Strategy Plan	Client Preparation Grid

Here we will look at how this is used and how important it is to plan for meetings ahead, rather then make it all up as we go along.

Why Prepare?

Success starts with preparation. We need to think about the Objectives of the meeting and what our *Single Sales* or *Marketing Objective* is.

Preparation really allows us to focus on what matters in the meeting and once we have set the objectives, it allows us to be able to evaluate how successful we were. Few people, in my experience, evaluate how well we conducted the meeting. To avoid this prepare in advance and set specific criteria in order to make an objective evaluation.

Preparation will help us formulate our views as where we are in the process of getting agreement with our client and what we need to do in the forthcoming meeting to move the project along.

This can be re confirming where we are as well as asking key questions that will help us obtain new information so we can get a feel for our customer's attitude about how things are progressing.

Remember, in most meetings of any description, we are normally looking to satisfy our customer, build long term relationships, ensure repeat business and obtain referrals.

What to Prepare

Good pre-planning enables us to establish our client's concerns and their *Notion*. I have discussed this in earlier chapters, but the *Customer's Notion* really is what the customer is thinking about a variety of things.

Everything should start with the *Customer's Notion*, because unless we understand that, it's unlikely we are going to be able to meet their needs - as we simply don't know what they are.

In Chapter Three we looked at various Customer or *Decision Influencers* such as **roles, support, degree of influence** and **mode** in order to help us get a snapshot of our customer situation. These form the basis of the *Customer's Notion*, but now we need to know more.

The *Customer's Notion* can include a multitude of things such as; what could your products, services or ideas do to help their company or their career? What problems have they? How can we help them solve their problems? What is the added value over and above competition? (And competition should be defined much wider than just another company with a similar product. Competition could be a completely different solution).

What do they think of you and your company? How ambitious are they? What's their career plan? **We need to understand their business and understand them.**

Here's a sample list of things that could be going on in their heads that concern them:

- Needs
- Wants
- Pressures
- Anxieties
- Stress
- Fears
- Concerns
- Wins
- Losses
- Risk aversions
- Insecurities
- Need for results

Now we don't need to become their therapist, although I can think of many instances where that would have been a distinct advantage. It clearly would have added value. But, we do need have an understanding of certain pain points and what success would look like to them.

Secondly, we need to be very clear about what our business objective and *Goals* are for the meeting.

What are we trying to achieve? It needs to be succinct and include the following criteria; it should be product, service or idea related, be specific, clear and concise, definable and measurable and tied to a timeline. For example:

To sell **Digital Technology**   **our XZ4567 servers**
        company/specific area   *product/service/idea*

for **$40 million**   **by** **November 2016**
    sales revenue/other units/new idea   *close date*

It is critical to be very clear about who we are talking to and their needs and then match them to with what our objectives are.

Now we need to have a scale for success of our *Goals* and these are what I term **Best Action Outcome** and **Minimum Acceptable Action.**

The best way to define the *Best Action Outcome* is to ask ourselves, "What is the best commitment to action I can expect this client to make as a result of this meeting?"

So, the objective we have set ourselves above should be the overall objective for this client for the year. Our *Best Action Outcome*, is what I can I achieve in THIS meeting that will help us move towards achieving our overall objective.

Here's an example:

Agree that XZ4567 servers are the right product and that the budget is in the $30-50 million range.

Although many people set a goal or an objective, very few set a *Minimum Acceptable Action.* This is where we should look at what is the minimum acceptable action we can accept and still continue to invest in this product, service or idea?

If we don't meet our minimum requirements in meetings we have to seriously evaluate whether we continue banging our heard against the proverbial brick wall. Here's an example:

Obtain agreement that the XZ4567 servers are the right product to meet their needs.

If we are not meeting this minimum acceptable action then we must either decide to walk away from this client, if this is possible, or change the overall business objective to something that will be more reachable and/ or reasonable.

How to Prepare

So let's look at the *Relate* App. again and how it helps us in our meeting preparation. First we open the *Client Preparation Grid:*

Figure 15

Relationship Map	Customer Strategy Plan	Client Preparation Grid

And then we start by *Understanding Your Customer.* Here we can enter a few details and can start typing in notes about our *Client's Notion,* such as the information I suggested above.

Figure 16:

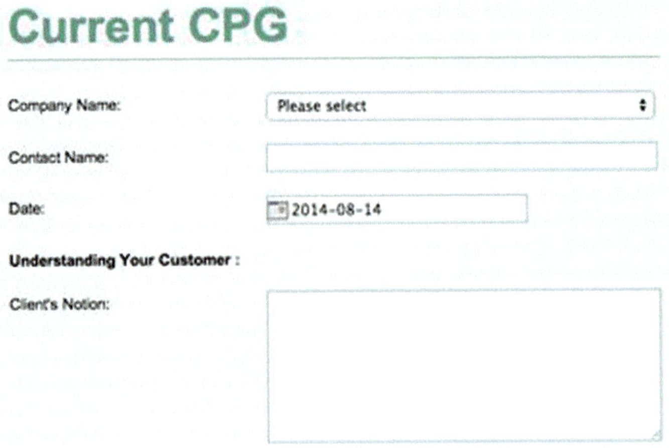

Current CPG

Company Name:	Please select ⬍
Contact Name:	
Date:	📅 2014-08-14
Understanding Your Customer :	
Client's Notion:	

When we are happy with that we can move on to *Understanding Your Goals.* Here's where the *Single Sales* or *Single Marketing Objective* goes that I provided an example for, above.

And then we start to add our *Best Action Outcome* and *Minimum Acceptable Action.* Whilst doing this, we should be asking ourselves whether this focus on the customer's action, whether that action can be measured, is the action reasonable at the point of where we are in the project and does it move things forward.

As we add bullet points and just keep typing down, the App. allows for a continuous flow of words to be typed into the boxes.

The last section of the preparation entails thinking and planning about the information we want that either needs updating or is a gap in what we know. This could mean any number of things, but some examples are; has there been a re-structure since we last talked, have roles and responsibilities changed, are the clients objectives still the same, how is the customer feeling about the project, are they still committed so the same deadlines and so on.

Figure 17:

Understanding Your Goals :

Single Marketing Objective:

Best Action Outcome:

Minimum Acceptable Action:

Questions need to be prepared to make sure we ask them in the right sequence so they don't appear to be randomly thrown out when it suits us. So we need to think about what questions that best confirm information or reveal information we feel is missing. We need to think about the best way to phrase the questions so that we get the right amount of information feedback that we are seeking.

These types of information requirements can be divided into *Confirmation, New Information* and *Attitude* questions.

Confirmation Questions tend to appear first in the sequence because we ask these types of questions at the beginning of a meeting as it helps us build a foundation.

These types of questions can help us verify what we know about the *Customers Notion*, what the business issues are, provide clarity about the organization structure, determine the decision makers and help confirm data accuracy. Key words in these types of questions would normally include; still, now, remain, currently and continue. So for example; "So Jim, am I correct to assume that the project **remains** the same since we last talked?" or "Are we still talking about installing the XZ4567 servers that we have been discussing up until now?"

These types of questions can also reveal any gaps we may have in our information, which can help us move on to a *New Information Question.*

New Information Questions are fairly self-explanatory right? They help us to better understand what the Customer is trying to accomplish, fix or avoid. It assists us in updating our information and they will help us in identifying missing information. These are used when we want to explore with the customer what they really want to achieve and when we feel we don't have all the necessary information we need.

The key words used with these types of questions are quantitative descriptive words such as; What, Where, When, How, How Much or How Many. For example; "So **how** many of the XZ4567 servers do you think you are going to need?" or "Have you an idea by **when** we will need to have the servers installed?"

Very often, we need to pries new information out of our contact. In that case we would be using words such as; Elaborate, Show Me, Explain to me, Describe to Me, Demonstrate or Tell Me. For example; "Can you please explain to me the reason for the timing?" or "Can you please elaborate whose now involved in making the decision?"

And so on to *Attitude Questions.* These are used when we need to understand **individual** needs, desires, concerns, and feelings. They help us discover any unidentified issues but they can also provide a better understanding of attitudes and the values of our customer. Often the real issues can be hidden behind objectives, goals and data, so we often need to turn to *Attitude Questions* to help us understand what's really going on in the clients mind.

So the key words that may be used for these types of questions could be What, Which, How and Describe. Examples using these could be; "**How** do you feel about the project so far?" or "Describe how success would like for you when we get things going?"

These words can also be used in conjunction with words that help the client develop and explain their feelings or opinions that will give us more insights about their viewpoint, such as: Opinion, Feeling, Reaction or Attitude. "What would be your **reaction** if we your management didn't approve the go ahead?" or "What is your **opinion** on the ROI numbers we've projected?"

So armed with these ideas and tips for the phrasing and types of questions that can be asked to help us move things forward, we can start entering into the App. a series of questions in the right segments as part of our preparation:

Figure 18:

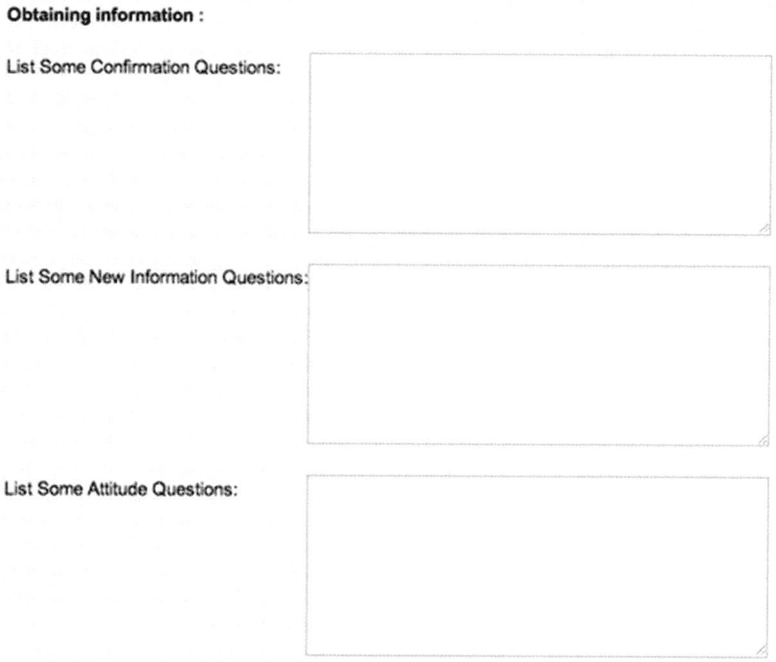

Obtaining information :

List Some Confirmation Questions:

List Some New Information Questions:

List Some Attitude Questions:

Lastly, we want to make sure we have an understanding of what will happen next, and so that we don't have those embarrassing conversations few days or weeks later, when we have a different understanding from our client as to what we agreed, we need to make sure we agree.

Years ago the expression *Closing the Sale* was coined, meaning that a sale was made. Lots of techniques were developed which were artful ways of persuasion and getting the potential buyer to say yes. One such example would be "Would you prefer the 2 door or the 4 door version of this car." In other words, offer a choice.

This kind of behavior is outmoded now and if we have had done our preparation correctly, we should be able to get a commitment simply by asking some *Commitment Questions*.

They are always asked towards the end of the meeting as a way of closure and determining whether we are progressing the right way. A sure sign of such an assurance would be getting the customer to agree to some action they have to take themselves to move the project forward. If that is not gained, then it may be we have to go back to one of the other questions and find out what the issue is.

A *Commitment Question* also helps both parties understand and agree what remains to be done. Once again there are key words that we would probably use in phrasing such questions, such as; Decide, Plan, Share, Commit, Direct, Schedule, Determine, Propose, Provide, Recommend, Agree and Secure. And an example; "Based on the **schedule** we have been through are we in a position for you to **commit** the budget today?"

So, having thought of some appropriate *Commitment Questions*, we would enter them in the last remaining section of the web App:

Figure 19:

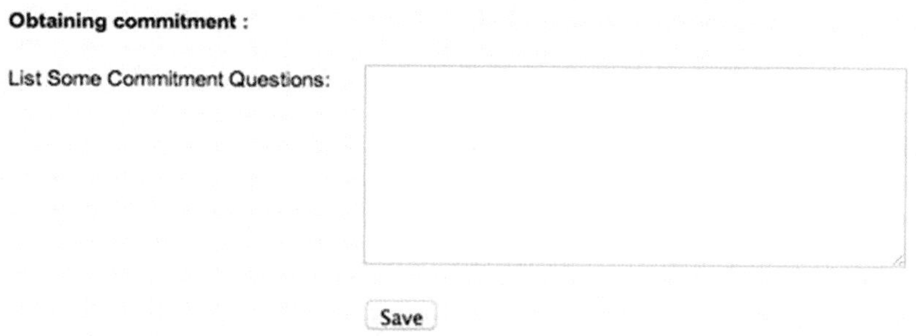

Obtaining commitment :

List Some Commitment Questions:

Save

Properly constructed questions, well thought through and raised in the appropriate sequence, can help us enormously in understanding where we are on a project, what our customer thinks of it, the likelihood of success and what needs to be done for completion and or agreement.

The App. is merely a guideline for what is a process we should try and use for any meeting that we wish to be productive. And let's face it; if we don't expect a meeting to be productive, then perhaps we shouldn't be at that meeting.

This process becomes instinctive and used several times with the App. we will find our brain starts wiring itself to the process and using it intuitively for every meeting.

SUMMARY

- Preparation really allows us to focus on what matters in the meeting and once we have set the objectives, it allows us to be able to evaluate how successful we were.

- Good pre-planning enables us to find out more about the *Customer's Notion.*

- Good, process driven preparation enables us to measure our performance of the meeting.

- We need to set a *Single Sales* or *Marketing Objective.*

- Having a Best Action Outcome and Minimum Acceptable Action provides us with a framework on which to evaluate where we are in the process.

- Properly constructed questions, raised in the appropriate sequence provides an understanding of where we are on a project, what our customer thinks of it, the likelihood of success and what needs to be done for completion and or agreement

- Using the web App. Helps us use a process that will eventually become instinctive.

ACTION

1. Before you're next meeting, block off 45minutes for preparation, where you will be alone and uninterrupted and have the ability to make notes or use the web App.

2. Make notes about what you think is going on with the customer you are meeting. What are his goals, aspirations and fears?

3. Construct your sales or marketing objective.

4. Think about the best outcome from the meeting and the least favorable result.

5. Construct questions that are *Confirmation*, *Attitude* and *New Information* orientated and think of some likely *Commitment* Questions.

CONCLUSION

Well I sincerely hope you have reached this page by reading through the book, at least most of it. Thank you.

I passionately believe in establishing relationships for the right reasons and that there is a process that I have laid out that helps us do it highly effectively.

Business relationships are too important to be treated merely subjectively.

The way the world moves now, we are bombarded with too many choices of media, too much e-mail, too many apps and too many pieces of information with insufficient time to properly consume, understand and deal with all of them.

So as with all things that matter, we need to prioritize, and relationships arc no different. In fact I would suggest that they are more important than all the other things.

Having the right relationship enables to get things done efficiently and effectively and to enjoy doing it.

I hope you took some good ideas from what you have read during this short journey through *The Relationship Roadmap*. If you have any questions, would like some support or just want to share some ideas, please do not hesitate to contact me. I'll do everything I can to help you.

My contact details are at the *Contact Peter* section.

RESOURCES

Books of Note

Selling the Invisible by Harry Beckworth.

Relationship Economics by David Nour

The Seven Habits of Highly Effective People by Stephen Covey

The New Conceptual Selling by Stephen E. Heoman & Diane Sanchez with Tad Tuleja

The New Strategic Selling by Stephen E. Heoman & Diane Sanchez with Tad Tuleja

The End of Marketing As We Know It by Sergio Zyman

Getting Things Done by David Allen

My Experience

My 40 year career, during which I was fortunate to work with brands such as Cadburys, Samuel Smiths, Express Dairy Foods, and then 21 years with The Coca-Cola Company and 16 years working on the McDonalds business.

My Key Confidantes and Mentors

Rick Nicholas

Mike Gerling

Johan Jervoe

John Gillin

Stephen Cobb

Mack Ketron

Neville Isdell

Muhtar Kent

Glen Steeves

Alan Pengelli

Chris Hawkshaw

ACKNOWLEDGEMENTS

This book is the result of my experiences over the last 30 plus years that have helped me formulate this Relationship Engagement process. In that time I have had a lot of help.

To take the concept and put it into a book was just an idea for several years and I would never have got it going had it not been for Alicia Dunams and her excellent *How to Write a Bestseller in a Weekend.* During the Virtual Bootcamp weekend I partnered with a wonderful Italian gentleman, who interviewed me as part of the process and who helped me enormously. Thank you Paolo Nagari.

Many thanks to so many people I have worked for and with that have shaped and influenced my career and views on business and life.

The best part of my career was when I was working for Coca-Cola on the McDonald's business and I lived in Vienna. The McDonald's Division at The Coca-Cola Company has to be one of the best run and most professional client service group of all and certainly the best I have ever come across.

Those were special times and I want to recognize just a few of the amazing people I worked with and learnt from and thank them.

My best ever client who became a best friend, Johan Jervoe.

To McDonald's from whom I learnt so much and I hope added real value.

The people at McDonald's that started with being customers and then became relationships that developed into friendships and who took their time and were patient in teaching me about their business; Mike Gerling, Branimir Lalic, Glen Steeves, Brian Weaver, Awad Sifri, Peter Beresford, Karl Fritz, Frank Mosher, Michael Heinritzi, Bane Knezevic, Khamzat Khasbulatov, Sarah Casanova, Tim Fenton and their very successful ex-CEO Jim Skinner.

The great example set by real leaders at The Coca-Cola Company that made real change happen but also understood compassion, Neville Isdell and Muhtar Kent.

Also with The Coca-Cola Company, within the McDonalds Group, the leadership of John Gillin and Rick Nicholas, the marketing expertise of Joni Hawkes, Kirk Thompson and Tracy Rice, the inventiveness, street smarts and loyalty of Stefan Thomas, Brita Stiegler and Steffen Kluepfel.

The dedication and perseverance of Werner Melzheimer, Mike Metz and Volker Bangel.

The amazing ability, adaptability and of course friendship of Stephen Cobb.

I learnt so much from all of you and others too numerous to mention. Thank you.

Every new business needs help and advice and therefore I would like to provide a special thanks to Cam Lindquist, the smartest person I have ever met. I have been fortunate enough to enjoy both his business insights and friendship as well as benefited from his and his companies expertise in developing my App.

Also, thanks to Thomas Ritchie, who got my website started and was a great sounding board on social media.

Thanks to Dale Willenbrink who has tirelessly edited my blogs and the majority of this book. An ex-colleague, golfing buddy and great friend, his professionalism and insights have kept me on track.

Thanks also to Carol Borzyskowski who has gone through the book again and picked up those annoying grammar, punctuation and wording details I wished we had changed on the first publication. Thank you for helping polish the final product.

And lastly of course to two of my favorite clients who have allowed me to put what I have learnt into practice…thanks Ryan Baker and Sebastian Siethoff and Matt Bireley.

If you think I've missed you out, my apologies as so many people have enriched my business career and my life. But I am pretty sure you are in this book somewhere.

Thank you all!

ABOUT THE AUTHOR

Peter M. Beaumont is a customer relationship expert who helps those responsible for their company's most important customers to identify, build and maintain the key customer relationships so they can protect and grow their business.

He has spent many years helping companies such as Cadbury's, Philip Morris and Coca-Cola succeed and expand through excellent customer relationship management.

Professional Background

He started his career with Cadbury-Schweppes in the UK in a sales position having obtained a Business Management Degree at East Hertfordshire University. He also obtained a Post Graduate Degree in Marketing while being employed with blue chip consumer good companies in various marketing positions.

Peter moved to Bahrain with Philip Morris as Area Marketing Director for the Middle East to pioneer new markets and consolidate market leadership. During his stay there for 11 years he re-joined Coca-Cola as Region Marketing Manager to pioneer the re-entry of Coca-Cola into the Middle East after its 22-year absence due to the Arab boycott. He travelled extensively in the Middle East, including countries such as Yemen, Lebanon, Iran, Syria, Jordan and all the Gulf countries.

Peter moved to Vienna in 1993 to head up a new Division of The McDonald's Group and help McDonald's (Coca-Cola's No. 1 customer) to build their operations in the Middle East, Africa, and India and throughout Central Europe. Appointed a Vice President, he travelled extensively throughout Central Europe, including Russia, Poland, Hungary, Czech Rep., Romania and Eurasia.

In 2004 he joined Creata to become General Manager of their Munich office. Creata is a premium sales promotion company and one of two that are McDonald's below the line Agency Of Record. Looking after Germany, Austria and Central Europe, McDonald's, Kellogg's and Coca-Cola were amongst the impressive client list. In May 2008, he moved to Head Office in Chicago for Creata and was appointed Vice President for Global Business Development.

In 2011, he was promoted to Senior Vice President responsible for Client Services, Strategic Planning & Communications to spearhead new management initiatives.

In 2012, he founded his own management consultancy company named ConnXN, which specializes in helping companies to measure, quantify, and leverage their relationships, thereby increasing their revenue and profit opportunities.

Personal Background

Born in England, Peter played district and county level schoolboy cricket, basketball, rugby and football for Hertfordshire. He was also an impressive opening batsman for Hemel Hempstead and Hertfordshire at cricket and played semi-professional football (soccer) in the Isthmian League. He trialed for and has always supported Tottenham Hotspur, one of the leading teams of the English premier League.

He is the proud father of a 31-year-old son who graduated with a Physics Degree with Honors at Warwick University, in the UK he currently resides in Amsterdam and has started his own successful business.

Re-married, he has a 15-year-old daughter and 12-year-old son with his American wife Shelley and they currently reside in Minnesota. He works out, loves writing, follows all sports, especially soccer and golf and has an X-Box on which he mainly plays FIFA.

He took up golf 20 years ago and is now has 10.5 handicap, of which he is very proud. He is competitive about everything!

CONTACT PETER

I'm easy to get hold of:

Tweet me: @pbeaumConnXN

Via LinkedIn: www.linkedin.com/in/pbeaumont

E-mail me: peter.beaumont@ConnXN.net

Or check out my Blog & Website: www.ConnXN.net

Printed in Great Britain
by Amazon